Facing Fears Head On

Facing Fears Head On

Renate Reiner

RESOURCE *Publications* • Eugene, Oregon

FACING FEARS HEAD ON

Copyright © 2026 Renate Reiner. All rights reserved. Except for brief quotations in critical publications or reviews, no part of this book may be reproduced in any manner without prior written permission from the publisher. Write: Permissions, Wipf and Stock Publishers, 199 W. 8th Ave., Suite 3, Eugene, OR 97401.

Resource Publications
An Imprint of Wipf and Stock Publishers
199 W. 8th Ave., Suite 3
Eugene, OR 97401

www.wipfandstock.com

PAPERBACK ISBN: 979-8-3852-6820-7
HARDCOVER ISBN: 979-8-3852-6821-4
EBOOK ISBN: 979-8-3852-6822-1
VERSION NUMBER 01/07/26

Scripture quotations are from The ESV® Bible (The Holy Bible, English Standard Version®), © 2001 by Crossway, a publishing ministry of Good News Publishers. Used by permission. All rights reserved.

Photo Credits:
Linde Lou Photography–*Copyright © 2014 Linde Lou Photography All rights reserved. Used by Permission.*
Renate Reiner
Bernd Damm–*Fiddler*

Song Lyrics:
Do Not Fear–Olivia Ferguson–*Copyright © 2016 Olivia Ferguson All rights reserved. Used by permission.*

Even If–MercyMe
Copyright © 2017 Ariose Music (ASCAP) Universal Music—Brentwood Benson Publ.
(ASCAP) (adm. at CapitolCMGPublishing.com) All rights reserved. Used by permission.

Copyright © 2017 Tunes of MercyMe (SESAC) / All Essential Music (SOCN) / Letsbebeautiful (ASCAP) (admin at EssentialMusicPublishing.com). All rights reserved. Used by permission.

Copyright © 2017 Crystallized (ASCAP) (admin. by Music Services, Inc.) / Tunes of Mercy Me (SESAC) (admin. by Fair Trade Publishing c/o Essential Music Publishing) / D Soul Music (ASCAP) / Universal Music Brentwood Benson Publishing (ASCAP) / 9t One Songs (ASCAP) / Ariose Music (ASCAP) (adm. by Capitol CMG Publishing) / Letsbebeautiful (ASCAP) / All Essential Music (ASCAP) (both admin. by Essential Music Publishing). All Rights Reserved.

Grief Quotes:
From *Message in a Bottle* by Nicholas Sparks, copyright © 1998. Reprinted by permission of Grand Central Publishing, an imprint of Hachette Book Group, Inc.

All other quotes considered *fair use* or *public domain*.

For Doug.
If not for you, I would never have recognized my fears and the need to address them. Even now, the tears fall as I write. I miss you . . . so much.

Contents

List of Photos | x
Initial Thoughts | xi
Acknowledgments | xiii
Introduction: The Unexpected | xv

1. How We Got Here | 2
2. What Is Fear? | 11
3. Fears Identified | 19
4. The Burden of Fear | 25
5. The Fear of Loneliness | 34
6. I Belong to God | 38
7. I Am Redeemed | 48
8. He Is My Savior | 54
9. God Is Always with Me | 60
10. Promises to Claim | 67
11. Truth Remains | 72
12. Final Thoughts | 79

Just One More Thing | 84
Afterword | 87
Bibliography | 89

List of Photos

Figure 1—Doug and Renate | xii

Figure 2—Doug and Alex | 15

Figure 3—Stella d'oro | 26

Figure 4—Christmas Carolers | 39

Figure 5—Fiddler | 41

Figure 6—Old Table | 49

Figure 7—Reiner Family | 57

Figure 8—Candice | 61

Figure 9—House and Trees | 67

Figure 10—Cactus | 73

Figure 11—Gerbera Daisy | 80

Figure 12 Doug and Renate Wedding | 86

Initial Thoughts

Eight years ago, my husband, Doug, was taken to Glory. The Lord put these thoughts in my mind nine years ago when we walked his cancer journey. For whatever reason it needed to ruminate. I suppose I needed to heal before tackling the task of expanding my contemplations into a book.

Authors have written volumes about conquering fears and I wrestled with whether one more would be welcome. Family and friends encouraged me to write, though, and several even mentioned that my perspective would be appreciated.

So, as I sit to write, I want to be clear. While I pray my words help you with your own fears, and more importantly, your walk with Jesus, this work's purpose is different from others on the topic. This is my testimony of how God embraced me at the absolute worst point in my life and lovingly guided me through a dark valley.

The Lord forced me to face the fears I didn't realize I had and to deal with each one. He used his Word, his people and unrelenting circumstances to accomplish it. The way was hard, ugly, and didn't turn out the way I hoped. But I came through the valley of the shadow of death with the Shepherd by my side. Along the way, he sometimes prodded me gently with his staff. Other times he yanked me out of the crevice I had stuck my head in to set me on the path again. Eventually, my faithful Shepherd led me up to the plateau where the grass was green, the water was pure, the air was clear, and my enemy, fear, was behind me.

This is my story.

Initial Thoughts

Acknowledgments

First, I am eternally grateful to my Lord and Savior, Jesus Christ, for fulfilling his promise to "never leave me nor forsake me." (Heb 13:5) My Shepherd firmly and lovingly guided me through the most difficult journey of my life. I thank my children, Alex and Candice, for encouraging me to write a memoir when I didn't think my life was interesting enough to share. To the *Emerald Coast Writers, Inc.* group, my thanks seem trite. Diane, Patty (Mother), Vee, and Lauren, you guys rock. Your editorial contributions made for the best manuscript I could hope for. To the members of *Grace for Healing*, our weekly meetings provided the motivation to record my grief on paper. Thank you for supporting me and for allowing me to do the same for you. Each of you is precious to me. And to the Reiner family, you've loved and accepted me as if it were my birthright. What a privilege it is to be in the fold.

"When you're heavenly minded, bad news is just news from God."

Iris Hodges

Introduction

The Unexpected

"We found a mass," the doctor stated matter-of-factly at 7:00 a.m. on a Monday morning. My fifty-two-year-old husband, who had never been hospitalized in his life, had just spent the last three days in the Baptist Hospital of Pensacola, Florida. Even though it was a weekend, Doug was subjected to several rounds of imaging and endoscopy. The reason was doctors needed to determine what was causing him such debilitating pain every time he ate. We naturally thought his gallbladder was inflamed. We would never have suspected it could be so much more serious. A two-and-a-half-inch malignant tumor had taken up residence on the head of his pancreas which was constricting the bile duct making it impossible to digest food. It was also the source of his pain. Doug had cancer.

The doctor left the room so we could take the time we needed to absorb what she had just told us. As the door closed, I burst into tears—loud, wracking sobs. They were the kind that left me with hiccups as I attempted to compose myself.

Then, the sweetest thing happened. The young nurse who was overseeing Doug's care for the day came into the room and asked if she could pray with us. It had come up in conversations with the care team over the weekend that we were career missionaries in transition to a new ministry in the United States. I'm sure that's what prompted her to come into the room to offer up the most beautiful words of faith and encouragement I had ever heard. She

Introduction

asked the Lord for our comfort, for peace, and for courage to face the coming days. I remember her words all these years later.

We had just arrived from Brazil and were spending a few days with my parents and our daughter before we headed to Cleveland. Now we had decisions to make. The most urgent need Doug had was to open the bile duct that had been constricted by the tumor. Before he was released from the hospital in Pensacola, the doctors were able to successfully insert a stent which allowed Doug to be able to eat without causing him pain.

The day after his release from the hospital we were on our way to Cleveland. Our colleagues at the mission headquarters had suggested we go straight to the emergency department at the Cleveland Clinic to seek out a treatment plan as quickly as possible. Doug ended up being admitted there for a few days and underwent more testing. They put together a care team and treatment plan quickly. Doug began chemotherapy within a month of his first trip to the hospital in Pensacola.

We were perplexed, numb and moved through those first days like robots. We called the kids to let them know what we faced. We called brothers, sisters, parents, and pastors of churches that supported our ministry. Our mission family embraced us as we explored options, sought opinions, and cried out to God. Those first few days are still foggy and nightmarish in my mind as I recall how I went about making decisions and arrangements. Suddenly, I faced a mountain of fear and uncertainty that threatened to render me incapable of being the support person I needed to be for Doug.

Up to that point I didn't know much about pancreatic cancer. I had heard somewhere that even one-year survival statistics were very low. Questions ran through my head. *Are they going to send us home and call Hospice? Will chemotherapy be an option? What about surgery? Can we get that thing out?* I was in new and hostile territory. I didn't know what to expect and I cried—a lot. It seemed my eyes were perpetually red and swollen.

The next twelve months were filled with countless ups, downs and sideways. I learned how to give an injection in the stomach, to disinfect light switches and doorknobs, and to carry on with life despite cancer. I vacuumed up human hair mixed with dog fur. I applied lotion all over Doug's body after a shower so his skin wouldn't dry out. I massaged his feet with lotion twice a day to help with neuropathy. If he craved a certain food, I got it for him. And many, many times I just sat with him and kept him company.

As I look back, much of it is a blur. What are very clear in my memories are the constant anxiety and the knot in my stomach that never went away. There were so many days I just wanted to stay in bed and hide from my circumstances. Every morning I asked the Lord to give me strength for that day. Every day he did.

So many well-meaning people sent us books, cards and advice. They shared their experiences and asked if we had tried one supplement or a certain food. Someone even sent a cancer Bible with devotions for those on that journey. We were told to eat certain foods and to avoid others. It was a cacophony, not unlike being in the jungle with the parrots constantly calling to one another. And it wasn't that I didn't appreciate their efforts to help us; I did. It was just that my mind and my emotions were so raw I couldn't process so much information.

My Bible reading that year was unproductive. I tried to read some of the books given to me but I absorbed very little. I was always preoccupied with something else—usually Doug. The "noise" I dealt with daily overwhelmed every aspect of my life. Most frustrating to me was that God's voice was lost to me. I couldn't hear it no matter how hard I listened. He seemed so distant and I was afraid. I was facing fears I didn't know I had; fears I hadn't identified or acknowledged. It was time I dealt with them or I would be useless to Doug . . . and to God.

As I came to this realization the Lord brought Isaiah 43:1–7 to me through two sources un related to each other. The first was in the book *The Upside of Down* by Joseph M. Stowell. Chapter 3 addresses "The Terms of Engagement" where the author reminds the reader of God's presence. That's what I was missing! His presence!

The other came as a song written and sung by the daughter of close friends. She composed then recorded it on a CD (compact disc) and sent it to us. Her father handed it to us during a visit with

Introduction

Doug and said we would be the first to hear it. The only CD player I had was in my car so I listened to it one day as I ran errands. Her sweet Celtic voice came through the speakers in a haunting melody. By the time she reached the first chorus which said "Do not fear . . ." tears were streaming down my cheeks and I had to pull off the road to regain my composure. God had spoken! I had heard him clearly and it was time to sit quietly and listen. I spent the next several weeks in Isaiah 43 studying, dissecting, praying, and studying more. I absorbed the words of God to the prophet and to me. The result was me confronting my fears. I identified them. I recognized God's ownership of my life. I fully understood the redemption he provided. I claimed God's promises. Finally, I realized God is sovereign. He knows what he is doing even in the most trying circumstances. I needed to learn how to listen.

That journey was the hardest I've ever faced. Fears surfaced and I wanted to hide and give up. However, I couldn't because Doug needed me and I had important lessons to learn in trust. God used my husband's illness to remind me of his promise of restoration and redemption. I haven't questioned his presence in my life since.

"There is no pain so great as the memory of joy in present grief."
                                            AESCHYLUS

1

How We Got Here

DOUG AND I CAME from vastly different backgrounds. I grew up in the United States during the 1970s and 1980s. It was the disco era where illegal drugs were prevalent and sexual promiscuity ruled. AIDs was the most feared disease and many celebrities were affected. Rock icon Freddie Mercury of the band Queen contracted HIV and AIDs which eventually led to his death in November of 1991. He was forty-five years old. Many of the rich and famous, like Magic Johnson of the Los Angeles Lakers, became the spokespeople for prevention.

The microwave oven hadn't come on the market yet so we heated leftovers on the stovetop or in the oven. We went to the store to do our shopping whether it was for groceries or clothing. My friends put clothes for the new school year on layaway at K-Mart before the current year was finished. We went trick or treating without our parents and played outside until the streetlights came on at dusk.

America was a society of consumerism. The Walkman, punk rock, big hair and heavy makeup marked the era. The hairspray industry never had it so good. Cable television was introduced in the early 1980s. We were one of the first families on the street to have it installed in our house. A whole new world opened up to us with commercial free programming. HBO was broadcasting movies without interruptions. It could make for a torturous experience because bathroom breaks had been eliminated and the cable company had not come out with a pause option yet.

And then there was MTV (Music Television), a new concept in musical entertainment. We could actually watch the artists perform their hits in color and without binoculars. I happened to tune in the day MTV aired for the very first time and watched The Buggles sing "Video Killed the Radio Star."

We were a religious family, but we rarely went to church. We believed in the existence of God, Jesus Christ and the Holy Spirit. Christmas and Easter were the two times a year you could find us at a Lutheran church. My father would only attend one that was part of the Missouri Synod denomination which was known to be the most conservative group. We often received a visit from the pastor the following week encouraging us to keep attending. We usually didn't.

My father loved his beer and I couldn't remember a time when he didn't have one in his hand when he got home from work. The reality was we were living with a functioning alcoholic which made life difficult at best, downright impossible at worst. There was a lot of yelling, berating, tears, and especially anger.

The years I remember well are those we lived on Weddel Street in Taylor, Michigan, a suburb of Detroit known as the Downriver area. Our house was a sturdy, though small, brick structure that had been built in the mid-1940s during the post-World War II housing boom. We moved into that house just before I started junior high school so I spent my formative years there. I was a typical suburban kid in the early 1980s living the middle-class life doing all the things I shouldn't and neglecting those I should.

That all changed in November 1982 when I gave my life to Jesus Christ. My mother had made the same decision a few months earlier and was attending a Baptist church in our area. She asked me to go with her which I did even though I wasn't thrilled about it. Actually, I resented it. But I went to please my mother. The hymns sounded ancient accompanied only by the piano and organ. The pastor would preach for at least thirty minutes, sometimes longer, which seemed an eternity to me. Then, at the end of the service, the obligatory altar call was introduced during the closing prayer where those who wanted to know how to give their lives to the Lord would raise their hands, go forward and meet with one of the people waiting at the front with Bible in hand. The two would find a quiet place to discuss the gospel. The service was boring and uncomfortable. Boring because I didn't understand the preaching. Uncomfortable because I felt I was expected to react to the altar call.

One Sunday the assistant pastor preached the sermon and as he finished, he asked this question, "If you have asked Jesus Christ to be your Savior and know you will go to heaven when you die, raise your hand." I had to be honest and admit to myself that I hadn't. My sin hung over me like an ominous black cloud ready to release a deluge of judgment. I couldn't raise my hand. However, the Holy Spirit was working in my heart, and one evening in November, I gave my life to Christ. I was seventeen years old.

The Lord continued to work in my life and, in the fall of 1983, I was at Baptist Bible College in Clarks Summit, Pennsylvania to study to become a missionary. Doug was beginning his second year although I didn't meet him until the next semester.

As I mentioned previously, Doug's upbringing was entirely different from mine. His parents followed God's call to missions in Brazil and spent their lives serving the Lord and establishing churches. Being the youngest of four children, Doug's life consisted of boarding school in the state capital of Fortaleza, only going home for the occasional vacation. He attended two church services every Sunday and one on Wednesday for prayer meeting. His mother introduced him to the gospel from infancy and, at the age of five, Doug gave his life to Jesus Christ.

Life in Brazil the 1970s and 1980s was completely different from the US. Northeast Brazil, where Doug's family resided was considered to be quite backward at the time and made the culture divide vast and easily identifiable. The Reiners lived in this semi-arid climate where two seasons prevailed, rainy and dry. When the rains came, flash flooding became a danger because the ground was so parched from months of severe drought.

The city of Iguatú, Ceará, where Doug lived with his parents when he wasn't at boarding school, was a typical interior town. Cars, hidden within clouds of dust zoomed up and down the unpaved streets. Walls which clearly indicated the division between what was public and what was private, protected houses built of brick. Instead of lush grassy lawns, hard red clay graced the front yards. Sweeping then sprinkling the dirt with water kept the dust from entering the house on the breeze. Daily routines consisted of cleaning bathrooms and mopping floors.

Having arrived in Brazil when he was five months old, Doug learned to speak English and Portuguese at the same time. His family spoke English at home and Doug and his siblings attended an American school in Fortaleza on the northern coast. They went to a Brazilian Baptist church on Sundays and Wednesdays, but the academy followed the American school year. All the missionary kids formed close bonds with each other that continue to this day. These missionary kids created their own culture that was neither American nor Brazilian but a unique combination of both.

When Doug came to the States after his high school graduation, it took him several months to acclimate to the US. He never did become fully comfortable with American culture, though. He counted the days to go back to Brazil at the end of a furlough. This was even true during our own furloughs as adults. He missed Brazil.

It was my freshman year of college and Doug was a sophomore when we met in January 1984 at a mutual friend's house. We had been invited to watch the Super Bowl. I wasn't an avid football fan at the time, but I was interested in getting off campus for a while and enjoying something on television. TVs were expressly forbidden at the Bible college. I distinctly remember the Washington Redskins were playing the Los Angeles Raiders (yes, they were in LA at the time) because Doug was pulling for the Washington Redskins (now Commanders). In all my maturity I decided to root for the Raiders for no other reason than everyone else was for Washington. Well, the Raiders won handily, but Doug was gracious enough to give me a ride back to campus anyway. It was the beginning of a friendship.

He declared his interest in me early on, but it was a while before I came around. I had some growing up and spiritual maturing to do which took me the rest of the semester and summer to accomplish. By the time we came back to school in August of 1984 I was ready for a possibly long-term relationship. By that time, I think he had given up on me so I had to convince him of my sincere interest. We started dating in September of that year and never looked back. Once we were a couple, that was it. We would only move forward and never doubted our commitment to each other.

Doug and I soon realized we had similar life goals in that we were both interested in full-time missions as a career. We were also in love. Our relationship grew during the next two years and we married in August of 1986. Our life as a couple began back in Clarks Summit, Pennsylvania, where the Bible college was located, because Doug had a good job with United Parcel Service and I was finishing my degree in education. I had completed all the classwork and planned to do student teaching that fall.

Those first few months of adjusting to living with each other and learning how to be married had their challenges. Doug worked hard so he could pay off his college loans. His second shift job washing all the UPS delivery trucks paid well, but he supplemented the income with housecleaning jobs. As a result, his spiritual life suffered. Doug worked so much during the week that he had little interest in getting up early on Sunday to go to church. Looking back, I understand he was also a little frustrated because we had no concrete plans for our future in missions.

One evening in January of 1987 we received a long-distance phone call from Doug's brother, Tim, who was also a missionary in Brazil and preparing for furlough with his family. He asked if we would be willing to spend a year covering the ministries he would be leaving behind. It was the push we needed to start the application process with Baptist Mid-Missions and at the beginning of the summer of 1987 we were on our way. We hadn't been married a year, but I graduated with my degree and Doug's student loans were paid off.

This would be the beginning of nearly thirty years of ministry in Brazil. Our children were born and reared in Brazil. We worked establishing churches which included a church for the Deaf and later in support ministries. We ran an island camp which could only be accessed by boat. I home-schooled our children for several years and Doug and I were active in men's and women's ministries.

We were fortunate to have Doug's parents and his brother's families near enough to celebrate birthdays and holidays. Those years were not without heartbreak, though. Our fifteen-year-old nephew died suddenly when he was electrocuted while stringing Christmas lights. Doug's uncle, Ray, passed away after a long bout with ALS (amyotrophic lateral sclerosis or Lou Gehrig's Disease).

Our colleagues made adjusting to and living in another culture bearable. They taught us many things and we mourned when, after many years of dedicated service, they entered the presence of the Lord leaving a huge pair of shoes to fill. I always felt my feet were too small to be worthy.

We also witnessed the joy of marriages and the births of children. My own two children claim Fortaleza, Brazil as their birthplace. The Lord blessed with churches founded firmly on the Word of God and Brazilian believers to carry on the work long after we were gone. We are privileged to have been part of seven church plants, mostly as a support team filling in where needed. The ministry challenged and fulfilled us at the same time.

In December 2015 Doug was asked to consider a position at the headquarters of Baptist Mid-Missions in Cleveland, Ohio. He surprised me when he indicated he would pray about it. I didn't think Doug would ever want to leave Brazil to take up ministry in the States. I didn't question his qualifications for the job. He was the perfect candidate to replace the retiring Administrator for Missionary Finance.

We happened to be in the States that year to spend Christmas with my parents in Pensacola, Florida. The children would be joining us for the holiday. Our son in Winston Salem, North

Carolina would make the ten-hour drive and our daughter would walk across the street from the little house we had bought a year or two before. It was a good time to consider a change in ministry.

We were invited to have breakfast with the mission president, Vernon Rosenau, and his wife, Jan, to discuss the possibility. We sat at a table in a Cracker Barrel while Vernon addressed the responsibilities of the position and why he thought Doug was qualified. At one point the conversation shifted and Jan asked Doug about his health. We both said he was fine. His yearly checkup the following January 2016 led us to believe the same.

Before we made a final decision it was important for us to consult the pastor of our home church in Hamburg, New York, a few other supporting pastors, missionary colleagues, and Brazilian colleagues. Doug and I both respected the wisdom these key people had to share. Everyone agreed this was an opportune time to transition to Stateside ministry.

In just three months' time we sold, donated, and packed everything we had accumulated during twenty-eight years of life in Brazil. In April 2016 we boarded a plane with five totes, two dogs, and our carry-on suitcases. We landed in Miami with plans to spend a few weeks with my parents in Pensacola. Our daughter met us in Miami to help with the dogs which was a blessing. It made the trip north so much easier. All the while, Doug was not feeling well and he was being quite stoic about it. His conditioned worsened to the point where he asked to be taken to the emergency department in Pensacola.

Doug followed the nurse back to an exam room where a series of tests and a fainting episode prompted the attending physician to admit him to the hospital. His liver function numbers were alarming and he was jaundiced. A battery of tests over the next two days revealed his condition. Doug had pancreatic cancer. It had been exactly one week since we left Brazil.

The burden of circumstances would weigh heavily as we navigated the untested waters of cancer treatment and uncertainty. I was forced to recognize, identify and conquer fears I didn't know I had. An uphill, spiritual battle stared me in the face. Doug fought his disease valiantly but lost the battle for his body. In the end, though, Doug was victorious because he now rejoices in the presence of the Lord with those who went before him.

My story is not over as I seek to continue in the ministry to which God called me in Brazil and to share the great lessons I have learned while defeating my fears. The following chapters will give insight to my struggle and my journey. I clawed my way back to the surface of the deepest, darkest valley of despair and grief as my Savior gently prodded. And while the pain still plagues me, it no longer drags me into the undercurrent of hopelessness.

"Those things that hurt instruct."

BENJAMIN FRANKLIN

2

What Is Fear?

As Franklin D. Roosevelt stood on the platform of the East Portico of the U.S. Capitol building giving his first inaugural address, he stated, "The only thing we have to fear is fear itself." It was March 4, 1933. The nation was in the throes of the Great Depression. Unemployment was at twenty-five percent. The homeless population was growing. People were desperate and afraid.

Then Roosevelt came up with a plan, the New Deal. This was sure to solve the country's problems. It would bring jobs to the people who needed them most and everyone would have what had been lacking since October 1929.

When asked where Roosevelt might have borrowed the now famous quote, the First Lady, Eleanor Roosevelt replied, "I think he got it from Thoreau." Henry David Thoreau was a well-known essayist and philosopher who lived in the Pre-Civil War Era. It's said his writings impacted American history during and after his lifetime. The statement FDR borrowed was most likely from one of Thoreau's journal entries which says, "Nothing is so much to be feared as fear."

I've been thinking about those well-known and often quoted words spoken nearly a century ago. It's viewed as a statement of great wisdom. I suppose I thought so at one time too, but the truth is I've never quite understood its meaning. It certainly sounds like something a great philosopher would say, but it's one of those phrases I never really understood.

Fear must be defined to be comprehended. And fearing fear sounds like a migraine trigger to me. Fear takes different forms and affects everyone uniquely. It can be a passing tightening in the gut, or it can be a debilitating malady that consumes a person's thoughts and actions. But we still don't have a definition that satisfies every type of fear or situation.

Merriam Webster's Dictionary defines fear as an "unpleasant often strong emotion caused by anticipation or awareness of danger." When conversation revolves around fear, this is usually the kind being discussed. The definition is well worded. Fear is unpleasant and is often an all-consuming emotion. It's what causes the color to drain from a person's face, makes one break out in a sweat, and makes the stomach drop. Fear also brings out other sentiments such as anxiety, depression, hopelessness, and despair. It can be downright paralyzing.

So, what is fear? The dictionary definition indicated a sense of danger. Near the church for the deaf in Brazil there was an alleyway many congregants used to walk through. It was the shortest route to the church. It was usually dark when the deaf passed through the alleyway for the main Sunday service. Several times the Deaf arrived at the church having just been robbed at gunpoint. This scared them to the point they began to take a different route. That is the fear of danger. Anyone with a gun pointing at them will experience it. But not all sources of fear are so obvious.

Fear of the unknown is probably the most common type and we all experience it from time to time. We all want to know what the future holds, but no matter how we go about it, we can't know it. Some like to read horoscopes, others consult mediums, others pray. The stars or a person who claims to receive revelations about the future cannot accurately do so. And although it's always a good idea to pray, God is not in the business of revealing the future anymore. All the revelation he is going to give is in the Bible. No

What Is Fear?

matter how we look at it, we face the unknown constantly and it's not going to change.

Fearing fear then, seems to be a double-edged sword and even more hopeless to me than fearing something finite. I'm not sure what Roosevelt was hoping to accomplish with his statement but there must have been some in the crowd who nodded their heads and looked at each other as if they understood the platitude. However, in just a few words Roosevelt managed to trivialize the very real fears of people with very real problems and facing a very real, bleak future. I can't help but think he could have come up with something a little more relatable. But that's me and I may be completely missing the point. I'm going to have to explore it more.

As I think back now, fears have always been a part of my life. Scary movies gave me nightmares. Haunted houses at Halloween terrified me. Arriving in Brazil for the first time was unnerving as I watched people communicate in a language I had never heard. Then, a couple of months after our arrival, I discovered I was pregnant. I was so thankful Doug went with me to all my appointments. He offered emotional support, but he was the bridge between the doctor and me.

When the time came to go to the hospital to have my first child, I was afraid and felt I had good reason to be. I was in a foreign country with a foreign language I did not speak. A cesarean section had been scheduled for the evening of June 30, 1988, and I had to spend the day fasting. My pregnancy was at forty-two weeks and it was time to get the baby out because he was not coming on his own.

I had called the American nurse in town who was well known and often assisted with the births of the missionary children. This woman had said she would go with me to the hospital. My obstetrician had a good working relationship with her and always welcomed her in the delivery room.

My conversation with her did not go as planned as she was quick to point out the doctor had scheduled the c-section in the evening for his own convenience and that I should insist he reschedule for the following morning. This nurse also said she would not be able to assist because she had other plans for the evening. I hung up the phone feeling perplexed and abandoned.

A twenty-three-year-old first-time mother doesn't usually push back against her doctor's wishes. Add to that the fact she can't communicate with him, and we have one seriously nervous and frightened young woman. That was me.

The day had already been emotionally draining because one of our pioneer missionaries had passed away the day before. We had spent the month with Uncle Wayne and Aunt Elva at the mission guest house and witnessed his steady decline due to cancer. So, as we awaited a new life, they awaited certain death. We spent many hours with them and enjoyed many interesting conversations. The brain tumor had taken Uncle Wayne's sight and I often walked onto the enclosed porch to see him lying in a hammock listening to the Bible on cassette tape. He was a picture of contentment and did not fear imminent death because Uncle Wayne would be in the presence of his Savior. After Uncle Wayne's death the hammock swung gently in the breeze without a body to keep it still. The cassette player sat in the corner with the last tape he had been listening to. It was silent now.

The memorial service and burial took place the next day as is customary in Brazil. I went to the service but headed back to the house a furloughing missionary allowed us to use to rest. A nap would have been nice, but I was too worked up to sleep. I used the time to make sure we had all we needed for the hospital. The hospital provided nothing and I had to take everything for the baby, even diapers.

Doug went in with me to the operating room which was an optimistic move on his part. He normally fainted at the sight of blood. The doctor told Doug that if he thought he might faint he was to lie down in the corner. Under no circumstances was he to leave the room because he didn't want to have to worry about Doug outside the room with me in it. True to form, Doug got woozy and had the good sense to do as the doctor ordered.

What Is Fear?

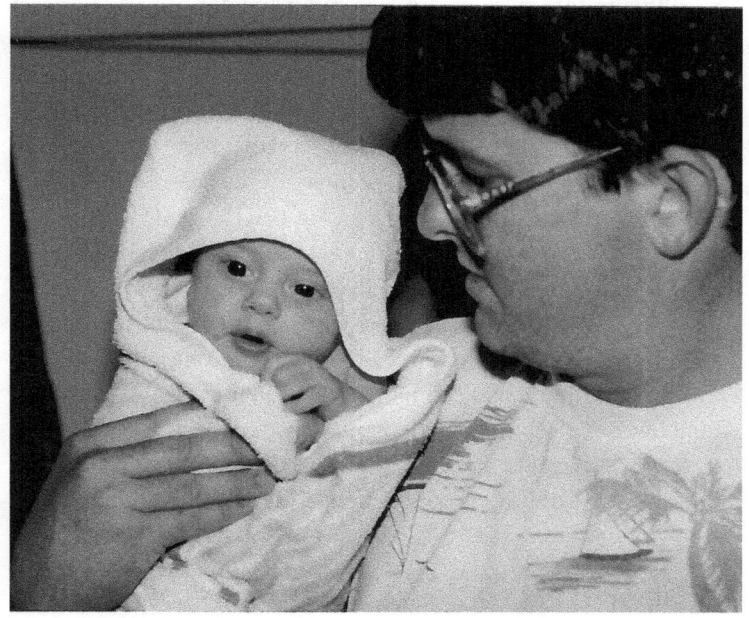

Once the baby was out Doug accompanied the process of weighing, measuring and checking his breathing score. Our baby, Alex, was then swaddled and Doug took him out to waiting grandparents. This was before I got to see him, mind you. They wheeled me out a bit later. When I went past the seating area, not only were Doug's parents there, but Aunt Elva with her son, Gary and daughter-in-law, Kathi, who was also pregnant and due in about six weeks. They were missionary colleagues and good friends. We couldn't believe they had come to the hospital to share our joy in the midst of their grief. Gary and Kathi's son was born six weeks later. Our Alex and their Joshua have been best friends since day one.

What started as fear of the unknown and uncertainty ended up being one of the most joyful days of my life. Thirty-seven years later we still reminisce about Alex's birth. That fear is the type that arises from external circumstances, threats, and perceived danger. In other words, it's a fear from a human source.

Facing Fears Head On

Outside threats played a role in an incident in the Bible in which a son of David feared for his life. Adonijah was King Solomon's older brother. He was also King David's oldest son at the time and tradition dictated Adonijah should be crowned king when David died. However, David had made it clear that Solomon would be king after his death. Adonijah staged a coup. He invited all his political allies and held a feast. He also took the opportunity to make sacrifices to the Lord which was common practice when a new king was anointed.

Adonijah failed to usurp the throne and feared retribution from his brother. Solomon was, after all, the one appointed by David and anointed by the high priest. When the people brought Adonijah to the palace for judgment, King Solomon had mercy on the would-be usurper and sent him home. Adonijah still feared for his life because Solomon could change his mind at any time and have Adonijah executed (1 Kgs 15—53).

The fear of the Lord is another matter because it does not have a human source. It is healthy to fear God. As Moses tended sheep on Mount Horeb he came by a bush on fire. It wasn't unusual to see brush fires in the desert region, but this fire was different. The bush was not consumed. When Moses stepped forward to check it out God's voice came out of nowhere. He told Moses to take off his shoes because he was standing on holy ground. Then "Moses hid his face, for he was afraid to look at God." (Exod 3:6) That is the fear of the Lord.

This type of fear can better be explained as a healthy respect for who God is. He is eternal, all-knowing, and more powerful than our human, finite minds can imagine. He is so powerful he brought an entire universe into existence with a word. He is so powerful that he opened the waters of the Red Sea for the Israelites to pass through on dry ground. He is so powerful that he brought Jesus back to life after three days in a tomb.

Passages in the Bible telling people not to fear are difficult to count because of the number of versions available. When God says, "do not fear," he is telling the listener to relax, everything is or will be alright. Isaiah 41:10 says, "Fear not, for I am with you; be not dismayed, for I am your God; I will strengthen you, I will help you, I will uphold you with my righteous right hand," meaning God has everything under control. The angel Gabriel, God's messenger, told Mary not to fear in Luke 1:30 because she had "found favor with God."

We all have fears. Some fears are logical, like meeting up with thugs in an alleyway and being robbed. Others could be labeled as paranoia they are so irrational. The fear of the Lord is healthy because it demonstrates our comprehension of his holiness and power. Recognizing the different types of fear and how we manifest them in our lives, aids us in identifying any that can be resolved by trusting God's mercy. As Paul told Timothy, "For God has not given us a spirit of fear, but of power and of a sound mind" (2 Tim 1:7). We should remember this verse is for us too. So, look those fears in the eye, and face them head on.

"Give sorrow words; the grief that does not speak whispers the o'er-fraught heart and bids it break."

WILLIAM SHAKESPEARE

3

Fears Identified

IF YOU'RE ANYTHING LIKE me, you may consider yourself a fairly independent individual who is not afraid to go off on an adventure, to learn a new task, or even make decisions with confidence. I am all these things. I love to travel. I love the challenge of writing a series of lessons for Sunday School. I don't overthink options when faced with a decision. Considering Doug's diagnosis, these characteristics weren't helpful . . . not one character trait aided in handling fear.

Even worse, I couldn't pinpoint the fears—I was simply afraid. Before I could begin the process of dealing with and eliminating these fears, I had to identify them. What made me afraid? What was it specifically that caused me to be so frozen with dread I couldn't move through the demands of taking care of a sick husband?

I had to look to the Word of God if I was going to successfully address what was distressing me. There is a wealth of comfort in the Bible, especially when I read the Psalms. David composed many of them and he acknowledged his own anxiety in several. He also used it as a platform to remember what God had done, not just in David's past, but in the nation of Israel's as well.

The first verse God brought to mind was Psalm 56:3. "When I am afraid, I put my trust in you." This was where I needed to start—I had to acknowledge the fear. I, the person who had left the security of the United States twenty-eight years earlier to be a missionary in Brazil, who underwent two unplanned c-sections in a third world country, who tackled the Portuguese language and learned to communicate with those who didn't speak English, was afraid.

David, the shepherd, wrote Psalm 56 when he was fleeing from Saul and subsequently, Achish, the king of Gath (1 Sam 21:10—22:2). He was afraid for his life and had good reason to be. Saul wanted him dead because David was a threat to his throne. David had been anointed by Samuel to be the next king of Israel. (1 Sam 16) Achish wanted David executed because he had killed Goliath, the Philistines' greatest warrior, in the valley of Elah (1 Sam 17). David faced so much adversity, yet his first instinct was to trust God. And he trusted God because he knew the Lord had a plan for him.

Sometimes, fear is not a bad thing. It's good to be afraid of the bear in the woods. It's good to fear those who mean to do us harm. Fear keeps us alert and demands we look for a way out. However, our fear should not consume and paralyze us to inaction. The remedy for fear is trust—trust in God and trust that God is on our side (Ps 56:9). He is the most powerful ally we can have because he defeats the mightiest armies. God heals the sick and comforts the broken hearted. And he does it because he loves us. We see it time and again throughout Scripture. And if God can defeat armies, cure diseases, and comfort the grieving, he can certainly teach us to deal with fear if we trust him.

It's hard. I know. Sometimes it appears God is either disinterested or unwilling to help us. He is neither. He's interested because he created us and loves us and he's willing because he gave his Son's life as a ransom for our sin. It's good to be afraid sometimes, but it's better to trust that God knows what he is doing when the worst of life's circumstances assail. Why? Because the Lord cares for his people and can be trusted. It's who he is. As I acknowledged the fear I faced, I realized I needed to be more specific in identifying why it was consuming me.

Fears Identified

When Doug and I first arrived in Cleveland from Florida, he spent several days in the hospital undergoing tests. He was discharged with upcoming appointments scheduled and a prescription list a mile long. Added to that was the fact we were essentially homeless. Things were not supposed to go this way. The plans we had made for our transition from Brazil to the United States were simple. We would rent an in-law suite from a couple at the mission office and immediately begin looking for a home to buy. Now, we had no idea what to do or how to plan. The in-law suite was only available for a short time. Another couple very graciously took us in and endured our daily drama for several weeks.

Eventually, a local church offered us a small house for a very reasonable rent. The house was tiny, but it was a place to have some privacy and it allowed us to live the anxiety without involving our gracious hosts. We had a place to feel somewhat settled during a time in which everything was so uncertain because each day was unlike the next. We didn't make long-term plans outside of chemotherapy appointments. It really irritated me that everything revolved around Doug's chemo schedule and even those could be canceled or postponed unexpectedly. I had become complacent by simply presuming the days would come and go and we would just glide through them without a problem. Suddenly, the future was never clear. It was scary to wake up every morning and have no idea what I would have to face in the next hours, days, weeks, or months.

One day, as I sat on the couch reflecting on my daily Bible reading, Romans 8:28 jumped out at me. "And we know that for those who love God all things work together for good, for those who are called according to his purpose." It's a well-known verse. Many have memorized it and cited this promise whether they faced mortality or the pitcher's mound. What does it mean to really cling to it, though? Well, to put this verse into its proper context, we need to look at the preceding and subsequent verses. Paul began the paragraph by speaking of the Holy Spirit who intercedes for us according to the will of God. He, the Spirit, uses language we can't understand. How many times had I not known the words to pray?

So many—too many to count. Thankfully, the Holy Spirit prayed the words for me.

Paul ends the paragraph by confirming these things work together so we may be conformed to the image of God. All things do work together for good. They also work to change me, to sculpt me into what God would have me be. He chips away the unnecessary bits and smooths out the harsh lines. It's a difficult and painful process, but, in the end, I look more like Christ.

The little house in Berea, Ohio was a blessing that summer of 2016 but it could get crowded. Our daughter moved up from Florida. We had brought three dogs from Brazil. Doug's sisters visited on a regular basis and we often had visitors from supporting churches. It was just too small.

One day I approached Doug and said, "I've been praying about it and I think we should look for a house to buy." Normally, my extremely objective husband would have come up with several reasons it wasn't a good idea. That day he just nodded and told me to start looking.

We eventually settled on the perfect house with a finished basement and plenty of room for three people and three dogs. Then we added my parents when I brought them up from Florida that December. My dad was suffering from Alzheimer's and was a handful for my mom. We all got along well and it was a blessing to have them with us.

Their presence became especially vital as Doug's illness progressed and I was home less and less to care for the day to day of the household. My mom made sure the house was clean, laundry was done, and meals were on the table. It relieved me of a rather large burden.

The future remained uncertain, but the Lord gave me a home and a family that would be my stability throughout the days to come. God knew I needed something constant to be able to endure the days ahead. It was a haven.

A few weeks after Doug's passing, my parents went back to Florida. I put the house up for sale and made plans to move to North Carolina. We had lived in it for only seven months. Some

Fears Identified

people had questioned our buying a house when Doug's cancer had such dismal survival statistics. I don't regret it, though, because for that brief period of time, we had a home again. As I reflect on Doug's encouraging me to find a house to buy; I realize he understood I needed something in my life that was stable. He knew me so well and was willing to forego objectivity so I could be settled. To share life with this man was truly my privilege.

"Denial, Bargaining, Anger, Depression and Afterward (instead of acceptance)."

SLOANE CROSLEY

4

The Burden of Fear

IN THE SPRING OF 2022, I sat at my desk which has a view out a large bay window. To my right is a large flowerbed in which I had been working since I bought the house five years earlier. I had pulled out daffodils that didn't bloom anymore and planted a knockout rose bush that gives beautiful pink flowers. I had added some black-eyed susans the previous year, but in 2022 I was trying to thin out the stella d'oros (yellow day lilies).

I retrieved a shovel from the garage and started digging and pulling. It wasn't long before I was huffing and puffing with sweat and hair clouding my vision. I put the shovel to the ground, placed my foot on it, pushed down and lifted. Then I moved a little to the left and did it again. What came up was a mass of dirt and bulbs. I banged the clump on the edge of the shovel, on the ground, on any surface that would loosen the soil. The bulbs were bunched so close together they didn't come apart easily. So, I continued to yank and grumble and wipe the sweat from my forehead. Eventually, I had a small cluster of bulbs and leaves. I stuck those back in the ground and covered them with dirt. The leftovers were given away or tossed. Stella d'oros are hardy and I knew they would take root, but in the meantime, they were going through the painful process of establishing themselves in the soil again. At the time, they looked a little sad and forlorn. The long leaf stems lay languidly on the ground instead of standing proudly erect. I was confident that a good rain would set them right.

In the early days of Doug's illness I identified with those stella d'oros. I had lived a life of comfort and complacency thinking my plans were going along just fine. Then, BAM! The Lord yanked me out of the ground, shook me out, knocked off the excess dirt, and plunked me back in to establish healthier, better roots. It was hard and it hurt. A lot. I was forced to remember the promise of Romans 8:28 and to believe it—really trust it. I was confronting the fear of an uncertain future and learning to hand each day to the Lord in full surrender. I had to trust his perfect will because God is good—always and in everything.

And those stella d'oros? Three years later they are ready to burst out their golden blooms and get the flowering season underway. I'll have to thin them out again next year.

While we were in the midst of our journey, I poured out my heart to God on Doug's behalf. Even so, the doubts crept in. I thought the Lord was not hearing my prayers because I just couldn't see him working. I prayed and pleaded and prayed some more. I would wait and wait with no answer—no change. This just increased the desperation and anxiety I felt daily. And it was escalating. Eventually, my frustration and impatience tripped me up and I came to terms with them because of a memory.

During our early years in Brazil, we could buy delicious fresh bread in the mornings if we were up early and the bakeries hadn't sold out. Sometimes Doug would rise early and go to the store to bring piping hot fresh bread for us to enjoy for breakfast. Any leftovers were stored in a plastic container. However, when I opened it the next morning, I discovered little rubbery loaves that would stick to our teeth when we attempted to bite off pieces to chew. In another day or two the bread would be hard as a rock. We learned to buy enough bread for the day or go without.

To us the bread was like the manna in the desert God provided for the Israelites as they wandered the wilderness. The manna would fall with the dew and was collected before the sun burned it off. The people had to be out early and each family was to gather only what they needed for that day—no more, no less. The Lord wanted the people's complete trust in his daily provision. Of course, humans are stubborn by nature and many gathered more than their allotment thinking they could store it for the next day. Upon rising the following morning, the Israelites would uncover the leftover manna to discover it had turned sour and was infested with maggots (Exod 16:19–20). The only exception was that they were to gather twice as much as they needed on Friday so they would have enough for the Sabbath when nobody was allowed to work. From Friday to Saturday the manna would stay fresh for the Israelites to use.

We loved tohave fresh bread so I thought I would make some from scratch. I quickly realized that bread making was not one of my better skills. The mixing, kneading, and shaping were no problem. I loved digging into the dough and watching it form into a nice solid ball that would sit in a bowl to rise. The first proof went quickly because the yeast was eager to work. The second rise after shaping took longer and I would stand and watch the dough, willing it to puff up into beautifully formed loaves like the baked goods advertisements. After an hour I couldn't take it anymore. I would light the oven and throw the pans in hoping the heat would give the bread one last push. Invariably, my loaves of bread were squat and dense—not great for making sandwiches. I was impatient and rushed the dough to a less than stellar finale. It tasted good though and we did enjoy it fresh out of the oven, slathered with melting butter that filled the air pockets.

One day my bread problem was solved. My mom brought a bread maker to Brazil on one of her visits. This wonderful example of inventive ingenuity could make a loaf of bread from start to finish. I measured and tossed the ingredients into the included baking pan. The paddle in the bottom would turn mixing and kneading with the right amount of time, speed and heat. Finally, it would bake a beautiful loaf of hot fresh bread that had risen to perfection. I simply threw everything in the pan, turned it on and walked away for three hours. I didn't have to keep checking on it.

The impatience of watching bread rise was the same impatience I experienced in waiting for God to answer my prayers. I wanted direction and relief. I was tired, confused, and anxiety ridden. I felt I was banging my head against a wall. God had never seemed so distant.

Once, as I was reading in the Psalms, I found, "Wait for the Lord; be strong, and let your heart take courage; wait for the Lord!" (Ps 27:14). I thought, yeah, sure, easier said than done. But isn't it just like the psalmist to repeat the key words? "Wait for the Lord." I took the chastisement to heart and concentrated on the wait.

Eventually, I established a routine of taking the days as they came. I would settle in bed next to Doug, praying his sleep would last the night. And I thanked the Lord for that day—even the hard ones. Every morning, as my red, crusty, sleep deprived eyes opened to face the new day, I thanked God and asked for the strength I knew I would need. Exhaustion was my constant companion but I learned the valuable lesson of waiting for the Lord to act.

In the meantime, I came to the conclusion that cancer treatment is brutal. Whether it's radiation, chemotherapy, immunotherapy or a combination of these it takes a toll on the patient and the family. The nausea, fatigue, and loss of appetite can be debilitating. While Doug was in treatment, I marveled at how much abuse the human body could take and still function. To give you an idea, the nurse had to don two layers of protective gear to handle the carefully mixed bags of poison that would course through Doug's body during a treatment session and several days after.

However, before Doug could be cleared for each treatment, he had to undergo blood tests to determine if his blood cell counts were sufficient to combat anything he might be exposed to afterward. Chemotherapy killed healthy cells along with cancer cells and he had to have enough of the healthy to protect him from whatever else he was exposed to. There were a few times his white blood cell count was too low to receive treatment. And there were several times he contracted an infection and had to be hospitalized. I had to be constantly vigilant in order to minimize his exposure to what could potentially make him sick.

I wouldn't let him touch public door handles. I made sure he had a straw for his drink when we went out to eat. Bottles of hand sanitizer were in every room of the house. Even through all the precautions, Doug was prone to illness. It was a never-ending cycle of being constantly on guard, and still, it wasn't enough. The possibility of infection was constant and unrelenting.

As the weeks went by the constant uncertainty and tension increased. I remembered a passage in 1 Samuel that Doug had preached years before. It's the story of Hannah, the mother of Samuel, one of Israel's greatest prophets. Samuel was, in fact, a Nazirite priest and the last judge of Israel. The circumstances of his birth, though, were the focus of Doug's message. Hannah was one of two wives of Elkanah. The other wife's name was Peninnah and she was able to bear children. Hannah was barren and she suffered for it. In a time when a woman's value was determined by her ability to have children, Hannah was considered practically worthless. Peninnah ridiculed her relentlessly (1 Sam 1:6). I can only imagine how miserable Hannah's life must have been. This abuse went on for years.

Elkanah loved her, though. We know this because she received a double portion to offer to the Lord at Shiloh. Still, Hannah was so distressed that she couldn't eat (1 Sam 1:7). Elkanah even asked her why she wasn't satisfied with his love for her (1 Sam 1:8). He obviously deemed Hannah worthy of his affection despite being childless. It was a good question, but not one that would bring Hannah the comfort she desired. So, she sought out the Lord in prayer and laid it all out in the open to God (1 Sam 1:9–11). Hannah acknowledged all her burdens and misery. She was so absorbed in pouring her heart out she whispered to herself. Eli, the high priest and the one in charge of all tabernacle sacrifices, interpreted her behavior as intoxication and he rebuked her.

Hannah had not been drinking but was making a vow to God. One could even say she bargained with him. She asked specifically for a son, and if the Lord granted this request, Hannah would return the child to him. She would give her son to Eli to rear and teach him everything he knew of the priesthood. When Eli understood this, he blessed her.

Hannah rose from her prayer, wiped her tears and "then the woman went her way and ate, and her face was no longer sad" (1 Sam 1:18). Her circumstances had not changed but her heart had. She went home not knowing if the Lord would answer her prayer or not. Hannah was in the same condition in which she had arrived at Shiloh: barren and childless. We know later that she did conceive a son named Samuel and she followed through on her promise to the Lord, giving Samuel back to be brought up to serve as priest.

I identified with Hannah because my own circumstances were unrelenting. I was tired, beaten down, depressed, and anxious. And I did the only thing I knew to do. I had to lay it all out before the Lord, holding nothing back. I let him know my distress, my hurt, even my anger. I told him my desires. For a while, it seemed he would answer my prayers according to my desires. Then, something else would happen. Doug would end up in the hospital again with an infection, he would have a bout with severe pain, or post-chemo side effects would take hold making him especially miserable.

Hospital stays could be especially trying. Doug was admitted several times because of a blood infection. This often involved several days of antibiotics and closely monitoring his white cell counts. He would only be discharged when levels normalized.

One time, Doug had been put in a room with another patient. I was sound asleep in the recliner next to his bed when a group of four nurses and aides filed into the room and started preparations to move him to another room. Bewildered, I asked what was going on. The other patient in the room had tested positive for the flu.

I gathered our belongings as quickly as I could manage amid the flurry of activity to move IV bags for transport and all the other lines and probes attached to Doug's body. I shuffled behind the procession still trying to wake up enough to comprehend what was happening. Doug was delivered to a private room on a different floor where he wouldn't be exposed to any infectious diseases.

It was too late, though. The next day, Doug had flu symptoms which extended his stay. From then on, I insisted on a private room for him any time he was hospitalized. It was the burden I bore throughout his illness and it amplified my fears of the unknown and unrelenting pressures of caring for someone with cancer.

When I think about how much time I spent digging up clumps of flower bulbs, breaking them apart, discarding the unnecessary, and replanting a smaller cluster, it occurs to me this is what God was doing with me. I needed to be shaken and broken apart to remove the obsession with constantly trying to do everything right to ensure successful treatment for Doug. I was carrying a burden that wasn't mine to bear. The Lord was in control and he would determine the result, not me.

Facing Fears Head On

Finally, I surrendered and quit trying so hard to maintain my grasp on everything. With that, God took my thinned-out root bulbs and planted me back in the ground. I lay limp in seeming defeat until the gentle, nourishing rain of God's Word refreshed my weary soul and body. I could flourish again.

"Without you in my arms, I feel an emptiness in my soul. I find myself searching the crowds for your face—I know it's an impossibility, but I cannot help myself."

NICHOLAS SPARKS 'MESSAGE IN A BOTTLE'

5

The Fear of Loneliness

The treatment process took a toll on Doug's body and mind which meant that I needed to be even more involved in making financial, healthcare, and family decisions. Taking charge of household finances and investments was not daunting. I was aware of what we had in assets, what our budget was and where our investments were. I knew how to manage all our accounts. We had a running family joke that we liked to tell. It was that Doug and I had agreed before we were married that he would handle the finances, the maintenance on the car and our home, etc. I would handle the kids' education, the day to day running of the house, and take care of the family.

One day, shortly after he was diagnosed with cancer, I came home from the grocery store and broke down crying. I confessed to Doug that I hated doing the shopping by myself. It seemed odd for that incident to be the one to set me off. I had done the grocery shopping by myself for most of our married life. Why was it suddenly an issue? I came to the realization I was afraid of being left alone to fend for myself. I may have done the shopping by myself, but Doug had always been there to help me unload and put everything away.

The Fear of Loneliness

Of course, I was overwhelmed with the emotions of dealing with a life-threatening disease and the uncharted waters of cancer treatment. Throw into the mix not having a permanent home, the transition to life in the USA, and the amount of information I had to absorb every time we were at the Cleveland Clinic. The result was one hot mess that was me. It was too much to handle on my own—or so I thought. I was afraid of widowhood and loneliness. I couldn't bear the thought of the grief I knew I would experience and was sure I wouldn't survive.

Then the Lord reminded me of his promise to "never leave me" in Hebrews 13:5. I had always been confident of this as it related to my salvation, but it was difficult to grasp during the uncertainty of cancer treatment and the unsettledness of not having a home. The sense that God might be distancing himself from me was constantly present.

Reading both verses five and six of Hebrews 13 put the idea into a better context. "Keep your life free from love of money, and be content with what you have, for he has said, "I will never leave you nor forsake you. So we can confidently say, 'The Lord is my helper; I will not fear; what can man do to me?'" (Heb 13:5–6).

The first two phrases were an indictment. I was covetous of the lifestyle we had enjoyed when we were healthy. We had never confronted anything as serious as cancer. We had our share of challenges, but we had never been so boldly threatened with mortality before. A feeling of discontent was also on my list of transgressions. It was natural to be unhappy with how things were. I longed for relief from the tension. I wished I didn't have to expend so much energy advocating for Doug, but if I didn't, he would not get the treatment he needed so desperately.

Hebrews 13:6 rounds out the thought with, "I will never leave you . . ." The statement was like a cooler of Gatorade dumped unceremoniously over my head. It shocked me right out of my immobility.

Hebrews 13:6 is a reference to Psalm 27:1 when David was pursued by enemies and running for his life. David seemed to be always fighting foes whether they were lions, giants, kings or even his own son. Every one of those circumstances drove him to trust the Lord. He rarely wavered from his faith in God. David's confidence in the Lord's presence and help was a striking example for me to emulate in my own dire circumstances. David had boldly faced the giant with a homemade sling and three smooth rocks from the river. One carefully aimed stone took down a nine-foot-tall giant as two powerful armies watched in disbelief. It took experience with a sling, the courage of a lion, and the humility of a young shepherd boy to bring an entire nation to its knees. David had all these qualities, but his resolute faith in the God of Israel was the catalyst in his victory over Goliath. That was the faith I needed.

The process of gaining that faith was excruciating and full of ups, downs, twists and turns. It was arduous, but I learned to trust God's sovereign, loving care and to wait for him to act. It was then I could reiterate Job's confidence when he was in the middle of his trial. The Lord led me through the blistering heat of fiery trials. And when all the impurities were burned away, I came forth as gold (Job 23:10).

"The term 'bereaved' feels so polite.
I need a word as crushing as the experience."

Unknown

6

I Belong to God

THE PREVIOUS CHAPTERS OFFER a pretty good idea of what I was facing at the time of Doug's illness and cancer treatment. My emotions were in turmoil. My relationship with the Lord was in question—at least from my perspective. I had no direction. As I read back, I realize it all sounds so depressing and the reader may be hesitant to continue. You could be asking yourself, *"Do I want to keep going? How is this going to help me face my fears?"* Let me say it wasn't all doom and gloom. We had many good moments and made some wonderful memories during that year.

Every photo taken and posted on social media was hash tagged #MakingMemories. I bought twenty tickets to the Cleveland airshow and all of Doug's cousins and closest friends accompanied him for the event. His brother even came from Brazil to spend that special day with him. My tiny house was full of men and boys. We only had one bathroom.

At Thanksgiving we went to Hamburg, New York. Doug's family had an impromptu reunion and we took over the basement of our church to have dinner. All the cousins lined up by birth order for a picture—something that hadn't happened in many years. My daughter, who was born on Thanksgiving Day, was honored with her favorite chocolate cake and candles. She turned 25 that year. All of us out-of-towners stayed at the same hotel so the party continued all weekend.

Both of our kids were home for Christmas and my parents had moved in with us. We had a house full of people, dogs, and joy. A church family surprised us Christmas afternoon by coming over and singing Christmas Carols at our front door.

In February we celebrated our birthdays with two other couples who also had birthdays that month. We met at a local barbeque restaurant, had dinner, exchanged gifts, and laughed a lot.

It was also during that time we received an abundant outpouring of love and generosity. The day we moved into the little rented house members of the church and our family showed up with a trailer full of furniture, bedding, towels, dishes—everything we needed to live comfortably. It was overwhelmingly encouraging. They were ministering to us in the most practical and tangible manner.

Later, when we moved into the house we purchased, our Ohio church family was on hand to haul boxes and assemble furniture. We were so grateful for everything they did to help us transition in the midst of our trial.

People were ministering to us in other ways as well and this is where the passage from Isaiah 43:1–7 began to have an impact.

Facing Fears Head On

The first verse declares God's ownership and the reason for it. "But now thus says the Lord, he who created you, O Jacob, he who formed you, O Israel: "Fear not, for I have redeemed you; I have called you by name, you are mine."

As mentioned previously, the daughter of a very good friend wrote a song based on the text. The recording she made opened my heart and understanding so that I could listen again to what God was saying through his Word. I've included the words of the chorus here.

> "So do not fear, for I have redeemed you.
> Do not fear—I have called you by name.
> O, do not fear, though you walk through the fire.
> Do not fear, do not fear, do not fear, My child."

God had caught my attention and it was time to get back to the Word—to spend time with the Lord and hear his voice again. My biggest realization? God had never abandoned me. I had always been His. He kept the promise to not leave me. That reminder was written right in the first two verses of Isaiah 43.

The passage begins with a declaration of God's creative work in making man and forming the nation of Israel. Then comes the statement, "I have called you by name; you are mine" at the end of verse one. God boldly says this to Isaiah and the nation of Israel because he has a redemption plan for the people he created and of whom he claims ownership.

My dad took up photography later in life and many walls in my home display his work. He even set up a darkroom at his home in Florida where he developed the negatives then printed the black and white photos he wanted to frame. One of my favorites is a shot of a Bedouin shepherd playing a single stringed violin type instrument on a street in Jerusalem. Papa snapped that photo with his manual Nikon camera while on a trip to Israel. He called it "Fiddler."

I Belong to God

As the paper dried and the image began to appear, Papa carefully cut a matte, centered the picture behind it, and signed his name. It's now framed and hanging in my living room. When visitors ask about it, I tell them it's my father's work. He was active throughout the entire creative process of bringing that image from its inception to the finished product. His signature is boldly displayed with his distinctive handwriting. Nobody else can take the credit for it—only Bernd Damm, amateur photographer.

When God says, "I called you by name: you are mine," he signed his creative work and claimed it as his own. We belong to God! We are his handiwork and he is proud of it. And this is the reason he can say, "Fear not, for I have redeemed you." He confidently declares, "I made you and I redeemed you. I've made a promise to you that I will keep because you belong to me."

Facing Fears Head On

We are set apart from the rest of creation because we were created differently. All of creation was spoken into being with just a few words from God's lips, "Let there be . . ." However, the Lord created man from the dust and then breathed life into Adam with his own breath. That marked difference is what makes it possible for us to have a relationship with God and it's why he claims us as his own. In Colossians 1:16 Paul states that "all things were created through him and for him." Make no mistake, we were created by God and we belong to him. That is enormously comforting when we face the mortality of a loved one. It's a precious and privileged position.

And the Lord doesn't stop with just that declaration of ownership. He qualifies it by stating, "When you pass through the waters, I will be with you; and through the rivers, they shall not overwhelm you," in Isaiah 43:2a. The prophet's words seem to reflect on the past as well as allude to the future. For instance, the first half of the verse talks about walking through waters. I would like to think this is a reminder of when the Children of Israel crossed the Red Sea during the exodus from Egypt. They looked back in panic as they reached the shore. The Egyptian army with Pharaoh at the head was in hot pursuit and it seemed the Israelites would be captured and taken back to Egypt. Moses approached the shore, stretched out his arms, and the water parted creating two great walls with a path in the middle. The Israelites then crossed over to the other side on dry land. More than a million people escaped to safety because of one gesture. No, it wasn't the outstretched arms of Moses. It was faith in the God who had created them. The Egyptian army charged into the seabed after the people, confident they would also reach the other side. God chose that moment to close the sea. The army of one of the most powerful nations on earth at the time was completely destroyed (Exod 14:10–31).

Isaiah then seems to switch gears and speaks of walking through the fire. "When you walk through fire you shall not be burned, and the flame shall not consume you. I will be with you" (Isaiah 43:2b). Isaiah was a prophet before the southern kingdom of Judah was taken into captivity by the Babylonian empire. Their king, Nebuchadnezzar, ruled the country with an iron fist. He also had an ego the size of Mount Everest and was the epitome of narcissism. When Isaiah mentions walking through the fire, he may have been referring to an event in Daniel chapter 3, which would take place roughly 80 years in the future.

The Jews had been captive for several years when, one day, Nebuchadnezzar thought it would be a wonderful idea to have a statue made of pure gold in his image for everyone to honor and worship. The king planned a grand unveiling celebration and summoned the people from all over the country. He also gathered a group of musicians. Nebuchadnezzar commanded that any time the music played, everyone should bow down and worship the golden image. Anyone who refused would be thrown into a fiery furnace, most likely a kiln for refining pottery. This would result in being burned alive.

In the audience were three young men from Judah who had been captured and brought to Babylon. They had gained positions of leadership because they previously demonstrated their faithfulness to God and the skills to guide the other exiles. Their Babylonian names were Shadrach, Meshach, and Abed Nego.

The king commanded the musicians to play and every person in attendance quickly bowed down to worship the golden statue—everyone except Shadrach, Meshach, and Abed Nego. They refused to bow down to an image made by man. They would only worship the one, true God who is not bound by human imagination (Dan 3:1–7).

Nebuchadnezzar's advisors noticed the defiance of the three young men and pointed it out to the king. They knew exactly how to manipulate the sovereign's ego and convince him to follow through on his threats. Nebuchadnezzar genuinely liked the three Jewish captives and gave them a second chance. When they still refused to bow, the king became furious. His narcissistic preclusions and arrogance proved stronger than his affection. He mocked the God of the Jews and ordered the fire to be stoked to seven times hotter than usual.

Shadrach, Meshach, and Abed Nego were bound with ropes and thrown into the furnace. The fire was so hot it killed the guards who tossed them in. It should have been a quick but painful death. What happened instead astounded the onlookers. A fourth being appeared with the other three and they were all walking around inside the giant furnace. Finally, the king ordered the men out of the kiln. The three Jewish captives stumbled out of the oven with no visible signs of having been in a fire. They were not burned. Their clothes were intact. They didn't even smell like smoke. But the ropes were gone, consumed by the fire.

What about the fourth being? Most Bible scholars agree it was the preincarnate Christ protecting Shadrach, Meshach, and Abed Nego from the fire and death. What's important to note is that God honored their faith and faithfulness by preserving their lives in a most miraculous fashion (Daniel 3:8–30). When the Lord stated the promises of Isaiah 43:2, he was making it clear that he is consistently faithful to his own. He is saying, "I did the impossible in the past and I will do it in the future. So don't be afraid."

However, the fire of my own trial was unbearably hot and it was difficult to sense the presence of my Savior. But he was right there in the middle of it with me. This became a significant learning moment for me. And the Lord used the pastor of the church we were attending to remind me that God is capable of accomplishing the humanly impossible.

By the time I was reaching this conclusion, my prayers were taking on a more desperate tone. Doug was struggling with chemo and his general health. I was asking God for a sign that he was going to heal my husband this side of Heaven. Trips to the emergency department became more frequent as Doug's immune system weakened. He was hospitalized with pulmonary emboli, sepsis, low hemoglobin counts, and eventually, a stroke. My self-confidence was shaken as I faced the possibility of being widowed—of continuing life without my partner.

One Sunday Pastor Spink was preaching from Matthew 12:38–42. Jesus was debating with the scribes and Pharisees . . . again. The Pharisees were the Jewish religious leaders and had spent their lives memorizing and studying the Old Testament, especially the law. These zealots were also always looking for ways to trick Jesus into contradicting himself or the principles of the Old Testament. He never did.

This time the Pharisees demanded a sign to confirm Jesus' claim that he was God's Son. The Lord responded with a rebuke. He knew they were not interested in a sign and told them they only needed to look to the prophet Jonah who spent three days and nights in the belly of a whale as the result of his disobedience. God had commanded Jonah to preach repentance to the people of the city of Nineveh. The whale spit Jonah out on dry land and, when he had cleaned himself up, he reluctantly obeyed God's mandate. Jonah's preaching prompted the people of Nineveh to repent and turn to God for forgiveness. With this example, Jesus essentially told those self-righteous hypocrites that the people of Nineveh were more righteous than the Pharisees because Jonah's message had the desired effect.

Jesus then spoke of the Queen of Sheba who came from Ethiopia to ask King Solomon questions about God. She went away satisfied and, as a result, many people from that nation believed God and his Word. Jesus concluded his argument by reminding the Pharisees that he, God's Son, was greater than Solomon and they shouldn't need another sign.

The Pharisees' demand for a sign referred to Old Testament prophets who often performed signs to confirm the words they spoke were from God. However, the Pharisees were missing the main point. Jesus *was* the sign. Furthermore, Jesus was the one who had given the signs to the prophets. The Lord used Jonah and the Queen of Sheba as examples of past signs. Jesus never sought to prove his deity to the people. He lived his life as if it were understood. He had already proven he could do the impossible. They had thirty-nine books full of signs the Lord himself had written.

The Pharisees didn't need more proof and neither did I. It was a matter of trusting Jesus was God then and is still God today. I have a complete book full of magnificent history and redeeming promises. I just needed to trust they were true for the past, present and future. God can do the impossible because he's already done it—time and again.

He's parted the seas, broken down walls, stopped the sun in its path, defeated great armies with only 300 men, brought down a giant with a single stone, saved men from the fire, and resurrected the dead. It's all recorded in the Bible which is trustworthy because it's his Word. This truth alone was sufficient for me to understand and believe the Lord knew what he was doing with Doug's life—and mine as well. The road ahead would not be easier, but it would be more bearable. Being one tiny example of God's creative handiwork is the most privileged position I could desire.

"We need never be afraid of our tears."
CHARLES DICKENS

7

I Am Redeemed

AN OLD TABLE THAT belonged to my grandmother sits in my garage. My mom likes the table and would like to have it in the house. Right now, it's not in very good condition. It has several layers of paint that are chipping in places and the table is a bit on the ugly side. But, if you look closely, a pattern is visible on the tabletop that indicates someone spent a lot of time cutting, shaving and shaping that wood to give it character. It's usable but not pretty. So, I bought some paint stripper and set to work removing all those layers. As I scraped, the wood pattern began to emerge and it's quite beautiful. When it is fully stripped, sanded, and stained the table will have been redeemed for a new purpose. It will be suitable for inside the house. I think it will look nice in the living room with a golden pothos plant set on it.

However, the table still sits in my garage a few years later, unredeemed. I see it every time I go out there and I say to myself, "I need to finish that." When it comes to redeeming people, I am thankful God didn't leave me in the garage neglected and unfit for being inside the house. This was true for the people of the ancient southern kingdom of Israel as well.

I Am Redeemed

According to Isaiah, the nation of Judah faced a grim future in captivity. Fair warning came from other prophets as well, like Jeremiah, but the people wouldn't listen. They scoffed, scorned, maligned, even abused the men God had sent to deliver his message of impending exile. Had I been on the receiving end of the declarations from these men of God, I think I would have been afraid. The people of Judah apparently were not. King Hezekiah even welcomed and showed diplomatic envoys from Babylon the nation's wealth in its entirety (2 Kgs 20:12–19; Isa 39:1–8). This just served to motivate the Babylonians to lay siege and conquer Jerusalem.

Even today, Israel is surrounded by countries and ethnic groups determined to take over their territory. Every news outlet usually headlines the latest events in the Middle East and Israel's involvement, whether direct or indirect.

Facing Fears Head On

At the time Isaiah wrote his book, the kingdom of Judah was steeped in idolatry and as far away from God as they could be with no interest in changing their rebellious nature. They may even have been a little smug in remembering the covenant the Lord had made with David centuries before (2 Sam 7:12–16). The people knew God would not destroy them completely so they carried on believing he would always rescue them from their own folly.

The people of Judah had been preserved and protected up until that point because of the unconditional covenant God had made with King David. It was unconditional in that the burden of keeping the contract fell solely on God and not man. Many years before, David received the confirmation that his descendants would sit on the throne of Israel through eternity. Every king of Judah after David was his direct descendant. (2 Sam 7:16)

Judah's rebellion would send them into captivity for seventy years, but the Lord would also keep his promise to David by providing redemption. God always had a plan and he knew how the story would end because he dictated and preserved it for future generations.

When the Lord says, "Fear not, for I have redeemed you; I have called you by name, you are mine" (Isa 43:1b), Israel had no need to fear, not just because of the covenant he made with David, but because they had been redeemed as the Lord's possession. God's plan for Israel was not without a promise. Their open idolatry had led them on a trajectory that would bring severe consequences but it would not be forever, nor without blessing.

Even so, the people strayed from the Lord's commandments and forgot all he had done. They preferred the tangible gods made of wood and stone to the One True God who is not bound by space or time. Finally, God had had enough. The people of Judah would endure a siege and then captivity for seventy years.

This is where redemption makes its appearance. Judah's captivity would begin in Babylon (modern day Iraq). Later the Medes would take over, then the Persians. Eventually, a group of exiles would return to Jerusalem with Ezra, a priest and scribe, to rebuild the temple. His obvious knowledge of Scripture would have been necessary in the construction process since the blueprints were in the books of the law of Moses.

Nehemiah, King Artaxerxes' cupbearer, would return with another group to rebuild the city wall after receiving news that it lay in ruins and Jerusalem was unprotected. The cupbearer's position at court involved much more than tasting food and drink before the king took a bite. He was a trusted adviser and could be compared to the chief of staff in today's terms. Nehemiah was a qualified leader and the best man for the job of rebuilding the city wall.

So, at the end of their exile, Judah was restored to its land and they were never guilty of idolatry again.

Although the kingdom of Judah didn't exist anymore, David's lineage continued and is recorded in the genealogies of the Gospels of Matthew and Luke. In the little town of Nazareth, near the Sea of Galilee, a carpenter named Joseph married a young virgin girl named Mary. They were both David's descendants. The miracle of Jesus' conception and birth was the apex of God's promise to David 1000 years before. As David's direct descendent, Jesus will establish his kingdom at what is referred to as the second coming.

Jesus' first coming had a different purpose, though. He came to be the sacrifice for sin. He came as our Redeemer. The sacrificial system set up in the Old Testament was a stop gap. A bull, without blemish, was an acceptable substitute for sin (Lev 4:1–12). The sacrifice had to be repeated when a person sinned and desired God's forgiveness.

However, Jesus who did not sin in his human life on earth, was the only one capable of bearing the burden of my sin—all man's sin. His sacrifice satisfied God's wrath once and for all because Jesus was never guilty of transgression and man would never be without it (2 Cor 5:21).

Romans 3:23–25 says it best, "for all have sinned and fall short of the glory of God, and are justified by his grace as a gift, through the *redemption* that is in Christ Jesus, whom God put forward as a propitiation by his blood, to be received by faith" (emphasis mine). Propitiation means Jesus' death was acceptable and satisfied God's wrath. He was the perfect sacrifice for sin thus making the Old Testament sacrificial system obsolete.

By his sacrifice I have been redeemed for a new purpose. The layers of sin I carried have been stripped away, and a beautiful pattern of redemption in Christ is revealed. Jesus paid a high price to provide us with the opportunity to be forgiven. He gave his life willingly knowing it was man's only hope of redemption (John 10:17–18).

Through this, the Lord has demonstrated his ownership with Christ's saving work on the cross. Paul asks a question of the believers in 1 Corinthians 6:19–20. "Or do you not know that your body is a temple of the Holy Spirit within you, whom you have from God? You are not your own, for you were bought with a price. So glorify God in your body." The cost of my redemption was astronomical because the burden of my sin was placed on Jesus who was innocent. His sacrifice negated the punishment I deserved (Rom 3:25; 1 John 2:2; 4:10).

I am redeemed! I have been given a new life to live for God who created me, saved me, and gave me a new purpose. This knowledge also provided me with the courage I needed to daily face the challenge of taking care of my husband. My standing before the Lord did not change with the uncertainty of my life, or even Doug's. I took comfort in what remained constant.

The pressures of Doug's illness and treatment were not as overwhelming. The uncertainty of what a new day would bring was not as intimidating. The burden of a future without a partner was just as heavy, but it was bearable. The hope of redemption did not change with my circumstances because my Redeemer lives! I belong to him and I have a purpose designed by my loving Creator.

While the illustration of the table in my garage pales in comparison to the redemption received at the Cross, it does allow us to visualize the concept. Christ's death and his subsequent resurrection provided my redemption. I am a new creation (2 Cor 5:17). I've been scraped, sanded, and covered with Christ's blood for his glory. I can now be inside the house on display without flaw or shame. And he stands back and says, "I did that."

"What soap is for the body, tears are for the soul."
JEWISH PROVERB

8

He Is My Savior

As a brand-new Christian going off to Bible college, I had no idea what I was getting myself into. It was a logical next step for someone expecting to go into full-time, vocational ministry, but I never realized my disadvantage until many years later. I didn't grow up in a Christian home, nor had I attended a Christian school. What I knew of the Bible had come to me as bedtime stories my aunt told me when she visited us when we lived in Germany. I don't recall anything that may have been taught during sporadic church attendance as a child.

While growing up, school had always been easy for me and I received good grades without much effort on my part. Textbooks were designed to build on the previous grade's topics so it was easy to segue from year to year. I went to public school so the Bible was, of course, not part of the curriculum, but those Bible stories my aunt had shared stayed with me through my formative years and were still in my mind when I graduated from high school.

Then I went to Bible college and lived in a dorm with missionary kids, pastors' kids, deacons' kids—people who had grown up in homes where family devotions, biblical discussions and church attendance were routine. I spent the next four years running several steps behind everyone else. Other students seemed to be in a refresher course for all the biblical knowledge they already had. The King James Version of the Bible was considered the most reliable translation at the time. I read it with little understanding.

New vocabulary, like the word "theology," was tossed out at me as if it were as common a term as "cat" or "dog." I was learning that the Bible was more than a collection of the bedtime stories my aunt had told me. Sometimes information came at me like water from a firehose. The rigid grading system the college implemented intensified my struggle to do well.

So, when I was confronted with new subject matter for which I had no previous base, the task became overwhelming and daunting. I realized college would require a lot more time and dedication to study than had ever been required before.

However, I preferred the social interaction and never did acquire the discipline of diligent study. I learned a lot, but it would have been more had I applied myself better. In May 1987, I graduated by the skin of my teeth with my bachelor's degree from Baptist Bible College of Clarks Summit, PA, but the years of life and ministry since then have taught me much more than any knowledge I could have acquired during college.

One thing I noticed during those undergraduate years, was that many students, even with a long history of Bible knowledge, struggled with their faith. They stood up during testimony day in chapel and talked about going through a time of doubting their salvation and about how God had brought them back from it. I think coming to know the Lord as a teenager was to my advantage because I never doubted my salvation. I didn't question God's love and forgiveness and I thought it odd that people who had grown up knowing that truth could question it.

Most likely, the circumstances of my life before Christ were different than theirs which made me firmer in my salvation security. It just seemed odd to me that someone could doubt the beautiful redemption provided at the Cross. Questioning one's salvation gives me the impression that a person is taking some of the responsibility on themselves—as if they may be losing sight of the fact that salvation does not depend on them, but on the Holy Spirit. It's his work, not mine.

Isaiah 43:3–4 claims, "I give Egypt as your ransom, Cush and Seba in exchange for you." This is a reference to the end of the seventy-year captivity when Persia received Egypt, Ethiopia and Seba as compensation for releasing the Jews. It appears that Cambyses, son of Cyrus, made Egypt a Persian province and forced Ethiopia to pay an annual tax to the empire. The involvement of the Sabeans is vague and uncertain. Basically, Persia was paid a "ransom" for Israel's freedom. The Lord had made promises he intended to keep and it was his work that set them free. God showed them a striking picture of redemption which alluded to the future redemption provided by Christ on the Cross.

Why did the Lord do this? They were God's chosen people. Verse four gives them three reasons. First, the people of God are precious in his eyes. He looked at his people, children really, as a loving father looks at his own child. It's a different look. There's a tenderness in his eyes that is reserved only for his children.

My husband Doug looked at both our children like that. When either of our children were nearby his face softened. His eyes especially took on a particular gentleness whenever he looked at our daughter, Candice. She could walk into a room without me noticing but I would know it was her based on how Doug's face changed. His countenance relaxed, his eyes lit up, and his lips curved up into a contented smile. He had a special love for his daughter.

Second, God's people were honored. The Hebrew word here indicates something that is weighty or burdensome which sounds a little confusing. I believe the weight or burden is the weight of God's affection for his people. As a parent, my children were always considered more important to me than other children. I am their mother. I carried them in my body. I nursed and cared for them as infants and nurtured them into adulthood. I will do things with them and for them I won't do for other peoples' children. I have a special affection for them. They are honored above others because they are mine.

Third, God loves his people. His relationship with his children is a loving one. The Hebrew word even encompasses friendship. I understand this concept better as a parent of adult children. When they were younger my love for my kids was focused more on their upbringing—teaching them to live godly lives. Now, our relationship is no less loving, but we talk more as equals, friends if you will. It's a different dynamic. My love for them has not changed, but I have the added privilege of being their friend now. That's how God sees his people.

We believers occupy the position of the adult child. He's still our Father, but he considers us friends. Jesus reiterated this in John 15:12–13. He gives the command for believers to love each other because someone who loves truly will give his own life for a friend. Verse 14 dictates who those friends are, the disciples who have accompanied him throughout his three-year ministry. If they had just listened a little more closely, they would have understood what Jesus was saying.

God also loves me unconditionally. His affection for me is not dependent on my obedience to him. Yes, I need to be a person, "growing in the grace and knowledge of our Lord and Savior, Jesus Christ" (2 Pet 3:18). But his love is not withdrawn from me when I turn my back on him. Jesus died for me because he loves me. My disobedience doesn't negate it.

A conversation I had with my daughter when she was about ten years old comes to mind. I don't remember the context, but at one point I looked at her and said, "You know, I will always love you no matter what you do or who you become."

She turned to me and replied, "Dad said the same thing to me yesterday." Within 48 hours, Candice received affirmation that both her parents loved her unconditionally. This gives me pause. It's overwhelmingly comforting to know that a child understands the concept of unconditional love. It is such a complex emotion, but even a small child can understand that it is a gift offered freely by the giver.

What Christ did for me on the Cross demonstrates all these characteristics. I am precious in his eyes, I am honored, he has an unfailing love for me. I did nothing. He did everything. My salvation comes from him and is dependent solely on him. I won't doubt it because I would be taking back the responsibility for my sin. He took that once, for all and left it at the empty tomb.

There are days I think I would like to go back to Bible college and repeat all the courses I took. I know it wouldn't be overwhelming anymore because of what I have learned throughout 38 years of ministry. Many lessons were hard. Others not so much. Each has served to mold me into the person I am today. So, no, I don't have to go back to Bible college. I need to move forward with my eye on the goal of becoming more like Christ every day.

What a beautiful Savior!

"Although it's difficult today to see beyond the sorrow,
May looking back in memory help comfort you tomorrow."
Author Unknown

9

God Is Always with Me

In September 2022 my daughter and I went on a girls' trip to Ireland. She had turned thirty the year before and it was tradition to do something special on milestone birthdays. For instance, Candice's sixteenth birthday was a slumber party and we invited all her girlfriends from school. I had compiled a list of sixteen things to do throughout the course of the night which included manicures, making individual pizzas and watching *It's a Wonderful Life*. The girls fell asleep one by one as we watched the movie so we had to finish the list the next morning. I think that birthday was one of Candice's favorites. So, as her thirtieth approached, I made a promise to take a trip with her. She chose to go to Ireland.

We wanted to set it up close to her November birthday in 2021, but there were still COVID travel restrictions in place and our schedules didn't allow for it. It crossed my mind on several occasions when we couldn't find a viable date for both of us to travel that I might have to back out of my promise to her. However, I had determined we were going to do this. So, we kept looking ahead in the calendar and decided that September 2022 was good for both of us.

Points with United Airlines bought Candice's ticket to Dublin and I paid for mine in May. The dates were set. In June her travel agent friend set up our sightseeing itinerary based on what

Candice wanted to do. It included overnight accommodations at bed and breakfasts. Again, points covered the car rental. By July, it was all paid for and it was a done deal. We were so excited and September couldn't come fast enough. I also breathed a sigh of relief because I had delivered on my promise. The trip was the most memorable we've had to date. And we had a blast!

I've always tried to be very careful about making promises to people because I know there is the chance I may not fulfill them. I'm human, sinful and prone to renege. But God isn't. He makes seemingly impossible promises and keeps them—every time. He does this because he is not human, nor sinful, nor is he prone to back out. He doesn't make them rashly. His promises are true because it's against his character not to fulfill them.

So, when God says, "I will bring your descendants from the east, and gather you from the west" in Isaiah 43:5, I had better believe it will happen. Isaiah was predicting the coming exile to Babylon when most of the people of Judah would be taken away as captives. The rest would be scattered to the four winds. However, the Lord promised they would eventually return, and after seventy years, they did.

As I meditate on this, I think the prophecy could have a broader spectrum. It's not unreasonable to believe the Lord is speaking of gathering his people again in the coming kingdom. There are many Jews in Israel today, but many more are spread all over the globe. Jesus will return to earth to set up his millennial reign because God doesn't forget his promises to his people. Furthermore, at that time, Jesus will bring all his people together (2 Tim 2:12, Rev 3:21, 5:10). I have complete and utter confidence that he will do it. Why? Because he has fulfilled every recorded promise so far.

This was important for me to remember as I waded through the waters of uncertainty during Doug's illness. The Lord emphasized these verses to remind me he is always with me. He had not forgotten me. He still intended to carry out his redemption plan and I am a part of it. I felt his presence again and was comforted.

What are the promises he makes in Isaiah 43:5–7? There are several. The first is the promise of security. God promises to bring the people together again. The natural result of this promise makes us feel safe and secure.

Think back to the pandemic and the weeks and months of "sheltering in place." Granted, we should be able to feel safe in our homes, but if we're forced to stay indoors we feel trapped, not safe. But we were also afraid to go anywhere—even church. We wore masks when we were out in public and avoided hand shaking or hugging. Our involuntary isolation was suffocating.

Everyone breathed a sigh of relief when restrictions began to lift. Walking into church that first Sunday after so long brought a sense of relief and security I hadn't felt in a while because my church has always been a haven. It's a place where I can worship, be spiritually fed, serve others, and fellowship with believers in Christ. It brings a feeling of security like no other and it's the natural outflow of God bringing his people together in worship.

The second promise is identity. We are "called by his name." For the Most Holy God of the universe to call me by his name is an awesome privilege. It's also humbling because I know me—all my faults and flaws—my sin. I don't deserve it nor do I fully understand why, but I'm infinitely grateful for it.

An account in Genesis 32:22–32 describes how Jacob wrestled with God. Jacob had been in self-imposed exile and was preparing to meet his estranged brother, Esau, after more than twenty years of separation. Jacob sent gifts ahead to be delivered before he arrived, then sent his family to another location so he could spend the night alone to prepare for the encounter. What happened was completely unexpected and profoundly life changing.

The Lord came to Jacob as he slept and struggled with him all night long. They physically rolled around on the ground for hours. Jacob would not give in under any circumstance. God finally dislocated Jacob's hip to stop the match. Still, Jacob held on and insisted on a blessing from the Lord. At that moment God changed Jacob's name to Israel which means "God strives or contends." Jacob, previously known as the deceiver, had a new identity which linked him directly to God. Later, the descendants of Jacob would be known as the nation of Israel. They identified as God's people, signaling to all other countries the Israelites belonged to the Lord. The Lord had given them his own name and they bear it to this day.

When we are born our parents give us a name which is put on a birth certificate. That piece of paper indicates our membership in a family and the name identifies it. Our family name gives us certain rights and privileges that others don't have. God gave Jacob his name which secured the association of every one of his descendants afterward. The Lord declared they were his own.

This declaration meant the captive nation could be confident they would one day be released to return to their land because they still bore God's name. This is the third promise. They would be gathered from the "ends of the earth" (Isa 43:6). Psalm 126 refers to Israel's freedom from captivity. It states they went home with shouts of joy. The promise of the still future kingdom of Christ can be included here as well. It's a done deal because God keeps his promises to his people.

I am not a direct descendant of Jacob but, this vow extends to me by the blood of Jesus, a descendant of Jacob. Jesus died so I could come into a relationship with him and become a member of God's family. I've been adopted which means the promises in God's word also apply to me. I anticipate seeing Jesus face to face one day as a member of the family of God even when the circumstances of my life are at their darkest. I have hope. It's not the kind of hope with the possibility of an unfavorable outcome. It's the hope of certainty and waiting to see God fulfill his promises to his people because they trust him.

Doug may have lost his battle with illness, but he will forever be identified as a child of God. Now, he is in the presence of the Lord enjoying the fulfillment of the promise. He is with other Reiners that went before and greeted those who came after because family is important. We receive comfort, support and love unlike any other relationship when we know we belong to God.

Speaking of the Reiners, I'm so thankful for that family. When I met Doug's father for the first time I was already engaged to his son. Harold Reiner walked up to me, gave me a bear hug and said, "It's so nice to meet you. You can call me Dad." So, I did. With five words he declared that I was now a member of the family as if it were my birthright.

As Doug faced the very real possibility of his death, he asked me to maintain contact with the Reiners. It hadn't occurred to me that I wouldn't keep in touch with them, but I suppose it's common enough. Nevertheless, I promised I would. And I have.

My sister-in-law, Jo, called just the other day and we chatted for an hour about anything and everything. Both of Doug's sisters introduce me as their sister, not sister-in-law. His brother is an older brother to me and we keep in constant contact. There are cousins, nephews, nieces and even a few uncles and aunts left.

We are family and continue to be so. That's a small glimpse of the promise of what is to come in eternity.

In the meantime, Candice and I have made a couple of other girls' trips since Ireland. We went to Mexico last year and met in Atlanta for Independence Day weekend this year. We're talking about our next destination and making tentative plans. Maybe we'll go to England and Scotland. I'm still cautious about making promises, but I live my life with the confidence of God following through on his because he is with me and always will be. I carry his name on my heart.

"The life of the dead is placed in the memory of the living."
MARCUS TULLIUS CICERO

10

Promises to Claim

I STARTED TO WRITE this book in the spring when flowers were beginning to bloom and the weather was warming up. Now, it's autumn and the leaves are falling. The colors seem particularly bright this year and the weather cooled off earlier than usual. I think we may be in for a hard winter. Hard for North Carolina, that is.

Facing Fears Head On

My yard is large in both the front and the back. The backyard has many mature trees that have grown tall. They're hardwoods, oak and maple, that reach toward the sky about 100 feet above the roof of my house. I estimate several of them to be over 100 years old. When the leaves begin to fall, they cover the ground completely and can be several inches high. As a result, I've given up trying to rake them into piles and have taken to mulching them with the riding mower. It's so much easier and the mulch serves as compost for the soil.

In order for the leaves to become mulch they have to go through trauma. As I drive over them, the leaves are sucked up into the blades and chopped into small pieces. Then they're spit out the side of the mower to make a nice layer of compost. If the leaves don't go through that process, they pile up knee-high and become slippery when it rains. Decomposition takes longer and the yard looks a mess until I can get out on the tractor to run over them. This process perfectly describes my state of mind toward the end of Doug's life.

Doug had a stroke on a Sunday in late March. It was the first time in my life I've ever had to call 911. Conversations with the stroke team at the hospital while looking at imaging revealed extensive damage. Recovery would be a long, hard journey. He spent about a week in the hospital, then almost one month in a rehab facility.

Jo, Doug's sister, came down from New York to help. She and I traded off nights sleeping on a makeshift bed on the floor of his room so he wouldn't be alone. Nights were long and hard because Doug never slept for more than an hour or two at a time. He was constantly restless and fidgety. Then morning would come and I would splash my haggard face with cool water, coax him to eat some of his meals, and encourage him through each exercise he could do. Intense physical, occupational and speech therapy were our daily routine.

I learned the proper way to stand Doug up from the bed and how to transfer him from bed to wheelchair. He couldn't walk on his own and didn't have the use of his right arm or leg. I watched him struggle to find the word he wanted to use then slur it out triumphantly when he remembered it.

Doug's improvement during the weeks in rehab was minimal. We took him home on a Tuesday at the end of April. Jo left for home a couple of days later. Rather than improving at home, Doug declined steadily. He would not eat, was constantly restless shifting from the recliner to the bed to the recliner again.

Friday night into Saturday morning was the worst. Our daughter, Candice, and I took turns sitting up with him as he was constantly trying to get out of the recliner. Doug eventually slipped out of it and ended up sitting on the floor. We could not get him back into the chair no matter how much tried to lift him. He was just too heavy and uncooperative. I told Candice to call 911.

The EMTs showed in record time, assessed the situation, and suggested taking him to the hospital. Candice and I agreed. They loaded Doug on a gurney and took him to the emergency department where he was admitted to the ICU. He was heavily sedated to keep the restlessness controlled. The doctors ran tests on Sunday and Monday.

On Monday evening around 5:00 p.m. the attending physician walked into Doug's room to speak with me. Our long-time friend, Bruce, was visiting. The doctor looked at Doug for a moment then turned to me and said, "When you came in here, I noticed right away you are a person that prefers to just hear what has to be said. You want answers. So, I'm telling you he is not going to survive this. He keeps stroking which is causing irreparable damage to his brain. All we can do now is make him comfortable." I didn't argue. I didn't deny. I wasn't angry. I was in a deep pit of despair and pain and the tears came immediately.

I handed my phone to Bruce and said, "I need you to call my kids. I can't do it." He nodded, took my phone and walked out the door. Within hours Doug's room in the ICU was filled with his children, cousins, nieces, sister, friends and our pastor. It was about 24 hours later that Doug took his last, wheezing breath and entered the presence of the Lord. Immediately, I asked Pastor Leary to pray for our family. He did. It was Tuesday, May 2, 2017.

Facing Fears Head On

At that moment, I felt like I had been chewed up and spit out just like the mulched leaves in my yard. I was living through serious trauma. A few months earlier we had been so hopeful that Doug was going to beat his cancer. Suddenly, he declined and I didn't recognize it for what it was—the beginning of the end.

We didn't stay long after Doug's last breath. We had no reason to because he wasn't there anymore. The body on the bed in the ICU was just the shell of what had once been a vibrant, healthy man. My son, Alex, and another family member took care of calling the funeral home and making arrangements to pick up Doug's remains. As I was leaving the room, I took one last look at the man I had loved and built a life with for more than thirty years and realized anyone walking by could see him lying in the bed. I marched back in and pulled the curtain around him. Satisfied, I walked out of the room without another backward glance.

For a year I had dedicated my focus completely on my husband. It is the most difficult year I have experienced to date. Circumstances had never been so dire, but the Lord led me on a journey of rediscovering the promises he makes to his children. I clung to them desperately because they kept me grounded in my faith and focused on what was important, my spiritual growth. I still count on them eight years later.

"The best and most beautiful things in the
world cannot be seen or even touched.

They must be felt with the heart."

HELEN KELLER

11

Truth Remains

It was June 1987 the first time I clambered down the portable stairs of a Boeing 737 into an oven called Petrolina, Brazil. I could feel the heat rising from the tarmac as Doug and I walked into the small terminal where his mother waited to take us to Casa Nova about forty-five minutes down the road. I was getting my first taste of the semiarid climate of northeast Brazil.

The airport lobby was sweltering and busy with activity as passengers crowded at a counter to retrieve luggage when it came through a door on the plane side of the building. Doug sat me at a lunch counter and ordered me a Coke. It came in a glass bottle with two thin straws sticking out the top which I promptly removed and took a long drink. I noticed people staring at me with open curiosity as I clunked the bottle back down on the granite counter. I didn't learn until much later that Brazilians don't drink straight from either a bottle or a can. So much for blending in.

I was receiving awkward glances from the people and soon realized that my light brown hair, green eyes, and makeup were distracting. I looked around for my husband and spied him making friends with the others waiting for baggage. I could tell they were all joking with each other as loud guffaws penetrated the din of voices. It was glaringly obvious I was different and I would be referred to as the "gringa" or "galega" (light skinned) for the next thirty years.

As I sipped my Coke, I looked around the terminal which was so different from any in the U.S. A couple of the walls had hand-painted murals depicting scenes of a biplane landing on a dirt runway with some men looking on. They were not great pieces of art, but they did reflect a time when aviation was a new form of transportation. The people of the interior regions of northeast Brazil benefitted from it because many towns were isolated. The roads in those days were dirt and poorly maintained making it nearly impossible to reach these tucked away villages. I took time to inspect the murals during every visit to the airport just because I found them so fascinating.

Doug came back fifteen minutes later sweaty and triumphant. He had all our suitcases which we piled into the trunk of Mom's black four-door Chevy Opala. Doug drove while Mom rode in the backseat. I was in the front passenger seat so I could get the full experience of riding down the two-lane highway because the windshield afforded the best view. The landscape consisted of scrub brush devoid of any sign of growth. It was the height of the dry season and the only green I saw was on the various species of cacti that grew like trees with three-inch spikes. They looked like they could pierce a finger with ease.

I realized I was in the desert and the nearest water source was the dammed-up reservoir several miles to the south of the road we traveled. It didn't take me long to realize how important it was to have drinking water handy all the time. Thirst could attack unexpectedly and clean drinking water was scarce if not brought from home.

The year of Doug's cancer journey was like being thrown once again into a desert and I had neglected to bring water. Everything had changed so drastically within days and I wasn't prepared for it. Many well-meaning people sent us books they thought would help, but it was almost impossible to read with any concentration. One book, however, caught my eye. The title, *Always True: God's 5 Promises When Life Is Hard* by James MacDonald intrigued me. I picked it up and started to read. The premise emphasized the truths that do not change no matter our circumstances. I needed to be reminded of these promises as I cared for Doug and later adjusted to widowhood. I soon realized that what remains constant, unchanging, could not be overshadowed by the uncertainty of the day to day.

The assurance that God is always with me brings me great comfort. "'I will never leave you nor forsake you.' So we can confidently say, 'The Lord is my helper; I will not fear; what can man do to me?'" (Heb 13:5b–6). God is not aloof to my problems. He is present with me in my best and worst moments and always will be. I know this because he loves me and sent his son to die for me (John 3:16).

Doug's cancer may have been a surprise to us, but not to God because he is sovereign and always in control. Some may ask me how the Lord could allow such a devastating disease to afflict a man who dedicated his entire life to preaching the gospel. I don't know. I know I felt Doug still had so much to offer this world, but the decision to declare his race finished was God's, not mine, and I trusted him to know and do what was best.

Job comes to mind because he was a faithful man of God who went through a terrible trial. When he lost his children, his livestock, and his servants within a matter of hours, he responded with worship and said, "'Naked I came from my mother's womb, and naked I shall return. The LORD gave, and the LORD has taken away; blessed be the name of the LORD'" (Job 1:21). Job understood that God knew what he was doing. God is sovereign, always in control and he is working every circumstance in my life for my good as well.

Many people quoted Romans 8:28 to me during that year. It says, "And we know that for those who love God all things work together for good, for those who are called according to his purpose." I would smile and say thank you, but in my head I was screaming, "I KNOW! It doesn't make it easier."

What's important to note, though, is that the next verse states the reason why things work for my good. "For those whom he foreknew he also predestined to be conformed to the image of his Son, in order that he might be the firstborn among many brothers" (Rom 8:29). Now it makes sense. My deepest trials are for my good because they ultimately make me more like Christ. My pain isn't lessened, but it's easier to bear because it conforms me to the image of Jesus.

How could I claim the promise and become more Christlike if I felt isolated, as if the Lord didn't see me? There were so many times I thought God had abandoned me. One time I broke down crying in the car and had to pull into a parking lot. Doug and I had just dropped his friend at the airport and we were on our own again. I was sobbing as I turned to him and said, "I feel like I'm walking in a desert utterly alone."

Facing Fears Head On

Doug's face took on a look of resolve as he seemed to make a decision. From that point on Doug was more like his old self because he realized he had been withdrawn and consumed with his illness and treatment. Although he never expressed it, I think he realized I still needed him to be my husband. I hadn't left the desert, but I wasn't alone anymore either. Doug was there beside me and so was the Lord. God used that moment to remind me he is neither blind nor deaf to my heartache by bringing my husband back from despair. I had found hope in the desert like a cool, refreshing drink of water.

This brings to mind a servant girl who had her own desert experience. Her name was Hagar and she was Sarah's slave. Sarah was tired of waiting for God to fulfill his promise to give her and Abraham a child in their old age so she told her husband to sleep with her servant, Hagar. A child by her slave would belong to its mistress so it seemed a logical step as far as Sarah was concerned. Abraham took Hagar and she conceived. Then Sarah became angry and couldn't stand to look at Hagar so she sent the girl away.

While the distressed servant girl wandered in the desert in despair, the angel of the Lord came to her, gave comfort, and instructed her to return to Sarah. Hagar's unborn son would be named Ishmael which means "God hears." Hagar praised the Lord in her response, "'You are a God of seeing,' for she said, 'Truly here I have seen him who looks after me'" (Gen 16:13).

I take heart because God never turned his back on me. He sees me in my greatest triumph and my worst defeat. He's right in the trenches with me and leads the way out just like he did with Hagar.

My son, Alex, signs his personal emails with a postscript. *In the end, God wins.* It's a simple yet profound truth. No matter what happens in this life, the end result is a victorious, sovereign Lord and I will share in it because he fights for me. "One man of you puts to flight a thousand, since it is the Lord your God who fights for you, just as he promised you" (Josh 23:10). My fears have no power to defeat me because the battle isn't mine, it's God's. His victory is guaranteed as I cling to the promise that when I leave this earth the pain will be gone, replaced with joy in the presence of my

Savior. One day, death will be defeated and I will live eternally with Jesus in heaven. And I will be with Doug again as everything from the year of facing fears fades into the back recesses of memory to be replaced with the delight of reuniting with loved ones.

So, as I think back on the day Doug died, I am reminded of the promise that God is with me. He is in loving control of my life and doesn't disregard my pain. Best of all is the assurance of being gathered to heaven to reunite with those I miss so much. Death is neither permanent nor victorious for the believer.

I've flown in and out of the Petrolina airport many times since my first arrival. It has expanded, is air conditioned and our luggage comes out on a conveyor similar to other airports. Coke is served in cans or plastic bottles now and I ask for a cup with ice when I order one. The murals on the walls remain having been carefully preserved during the various phases of construction. They are the reminders of what used to be.

The oasis of truth has relieved the desert's dry, consuming heat. I picture myself stumbling to a small pond of crystal-clear water and scooping up water with my hands to quench my thirst. As a result, my soul is restored and I'm better able to envision the Lord's loving care for me. The desert is still out there, but I'm protected in the oasis of God's presence.

"When someone you love becomes a memory,
the memory becomes a treasure."

AUTHOR UNKNOWN

12

Final Thoughts

EARLY IN THE SUMMER of 2016 I decided to spruce up the flower beds of the little house we were renting from the church in Berea, Ohio. I went to the Walmart Garden Center and bought a flat of petunias and pansies to plant. Because I am a consummate bargain shopper, I looked through the clearance plants for anything that might be salvageable and interesting. I found a green leafy plant that looked quite healthy but I had no idea what it was. It cost a dollar and I thought I couldn't go wrong. So, I bought it, took it home, and planted it in a pretty pot.

As I parted the leaves one day to add water, I noticed what looked like might be a flower bud. It was strange to me though, as the bud was coming up from the dirt at the base of the leaves. It was hidden because the leaves were quite full and large. I checked it every couple of days and watched it grow and break through the canopy. When it bloomed, I discovered it was a gerbera daisy. Then, I had an epiphany. The trial I was facing was very much like that flower's. Darkness was overwhelming and encumbered me with fears. The journey upward was arduous as I navigated the obstacles of fear and anxiety. When I finally came to terms with what made me afraid, I was able to break through, stand tall, and embrace life in the sun.

Facing Fears Head On

There are two takeaways I remind myself of constantly. First, God is sovereign in all and over all. When Israel was in captivity in Babylon, the prophet, Jeremiah, prompted by the Holy Spirit, wrote a letter to the exiles living in that land. He gave some instructions on how to live during a time of oppression. In Jeremiah 29:10–11 the prophet wrote, "For thus says the Lord: When seventy years are completed for Babylon, I will visit you, and I will fulfill to you my promise and bring you back to this place [Jerusalem]. For I know the plans I have for you, declares the Lord, plans for welfare and not for evil, to give you a future and a hope." God promised he would bring the people of Judah out of captivity because he had a specific objective for them. Nothing could prevent the Lord from accomplishing it because he is sovereign.

While we were around Doug's bedside that last day, a cousin played a song by MercyMe entitled "Even If." Its lyrics speak of

God's omnipotence, but the second verse focuses on his sovereignty. It goes like this:

> "They say it only takes a little faith
> To move a mountain
> Well good thing
> A little faith is all I have, right now
> But God, when You choose
> To leave mountains unmovable
> Oh give me the strength to be able to sing
> It is well with my soul"

My prayers and my pleas on my husband's behalf seemed to fall on deaf ears and made me question how much faith I really had. I hadn't ever examined it before, but as I faced the uncertainty of a future without Doug, it seemed to me that my faith in the Lord's power over disease and death had diminished.

The mustard seed analogy came to mind. The Gospel of Matthew tells the account of a boy who was demon possessed and suffered from seizures. They were so violent that the child often fell into the fire or the water. The boy's father took him to Jesus' disciples for healing, but they were unsuccessful in their attempts to cast the demon out. So, the father took his son to Jesus for healing. In exasperation, Jesus said, "'O faithless and twisted generation, how long am I to be with you? How long am I to bear with you? Bring him here to me'" (Matt 17:17). Then Jesus healed the boy and sent him on his way with his very relieved father.

The disciples were confused. Why couldn't they cast the demon out? Jesus replied, "'Because of your little faith. For truly, I say to you, if you have faith like a grain of mustard seed, you will say to this mountain, 'Move from here to there,' and it will move, and nothing will be impossible for you'" (Matt 17:20). The disciples were focused on the power to heal, not the source of it. They failed miserably when they forgot that key principle. It also demonstrated a lack of faith in the Source of the power, the Almighty God.

I wasn't trying to cast out demons, but in my desperation, I was taking too much of the responsibility to cure Doug's disease. I had absolutely no power over it. But God did. The amount of faith needed to believe the Lord's omnipotence over disease and death was minimal. And that little bit is enough to move mountains.

Here's the kicker, though. God is still sovereign over the mountain. I may have enough faith to move that monstrosity of a rock, but it will only move if the Lord wills it. Faith may be strong, but God's will is stronger and everything is subject to it.

While I listened to that song, I knew that my faith was big enough. The question was not, "Do I have enough faith?" It was, "Is what I'm asking within the Lord's will?" That took a tremendous amount of pressure off me. I came to the conclusion I was doing all that was in my power to do—have faith in God's sovereignty and omnipotence.

Then, another realization dawned. I had finally heard God's voice. And just like Elijah standing at the entrance to the cave, I knew the Lord was not in the wind, or the earthquake, or the fire. God was in the silence (1 Kgs 19:11–13).

As Doug was taking his final breaths we stood around his bed and quietly listened. The only noise was that of the machine monitoring his heartbeat. The beeping slowed until there was just the constant tone of the flatline. Then, mercifully, the nurse turned the monitor off. I was heartbroken, but I was comforted to know that the Lord had communicated.

God had torn my heart into pieces and put it back together again. If you know anything about welding you know the substance used to weld two pieces of steel together is stronger than the metal itself. If the steel breaks, it will usually be somewhere other than the weld. That's my heart today. It's stronger than it ever was because of the healing weld of God's Word. I feel his presence now more than ever.

And my fears? Well, there isn't much that makes me afraid anymore. The anxiety is gone and what's left is a trust that doesn't waver. The Lord had accomplished his will and I had done what was expected of me as a wife and a child of God. I had walked through the refiner's fire and claimed Job's words as my own. "'But he knows the way that I take; when he has tried me, I shall come out as gold'" (Job 23:10).

Final Thoughts

The years since Doug's homegoing have been ones of personal and spiritual growth for me. I've wrestled with loneliness and all five stages of grief, often revisiting stages I thought I had resolved. However, the growth I've experienced and new opportunities for ministry have contributed to making me a more effective servant of Christ. And that's the best I could hope for.

Just One More Thing

SATURDAY, AUGUST 30, 2025, was Doug's and my 39th wedding anniversary and I didn't remember. The last one we had together was our 30th in 2016. Doug had a chemo appointment that day. I don't recall that we did anything else.

As I was getting ready for church Sunday, August 31st, it finally hit me. I had gone through the entire day Saturday and didn't think about it once. I had thought about Doug. He comes to mind every day without fail. But I didn't think about our wedding anniversary.

The week before, as I was looking for my mom's wedding pictures, I remembered it was coming up. I even came across our own wedding album and debated pulling it out of the tote it's stored in, but I left it. I thought about our anniversary several times that week and meant to make a note to do something, but I was distracted by the day to day demands. Something more urgent would get in my face and say, "C'mon, let's get this done."

The tyranny of the urgent dominated that week. I participated in the funeral for an adult daughter of colleagues from Brazil which covered two days. Monday evening I watched three girls ages ten, six and four, the hooligans, while their parents attended a dinner at the pastor's house. As they were leaving, Scrappy, my daughter's dog staying with me for a few months, decided to pick a fight with a skunk. She lost. One week and three baths later I was still paying the price.

I was feeling all kinds of guilty and the irony of the whole sad story is that Doug and I were married on Labor Day weekend. The weather had been cooler than usual for late August in Michigan and the sky was clear blue. It couldn't have been more perfect. The anniversary I forgot was exactly like the day of our wedding—cool, perfect, and Labor Day weekend.

I probably shouldn't be so hard on myself, though. My life is full of enough obligations and demands to distract even the most focused of people. I'm not married anymore, either legally or spiritually. I haven't worn my wedding rings since Doug's funeral. All of my wedding mementos are tucked into totes in the garage. But not a day goes by that I don't think about Doug. He is the constant in my memories and I know the days will continue with him unfailingly on my mind.

So, I forgot my wedding anniversary. It was an important day, but only one in a lifetime of recollections. I remembered it on Sunday and enjoyed a little walk through the memories in my mind. I may or may not remember it next year. I won't stress or let guilt rob me of the pleasure of reminiscing . . . whenever that may be. It's good to recall the important milestones, but it's ok to forget them from time to time. They're part of of a bigger picture that is always at the forefront of my mind's eye. Every once in a while I'll zoom in, take a closer look and smile.

Facing Fears Head On

Afterword

THE OTHER DAY I listened to the recording of "Do Not Fear," Olivia's song for Doug. My mind instantly flooded with memories and my eyes with tears. But as Liv's sweet Celtic voice sang, I thanked God for promises fulfilled and fears conquered. I had to include the lyrics because they express exactly what Doug and I experienced, the hope we had in the redemption Christ provided, and the faith to believe.

Thank you for taking the time to read these thoughts of mine. I could not have written this had I not experienced the hardest season of my life. I am not bitter about it, but I've asked God not to put me through the experience again. I look back and see how it worked for my good, but it's a lesson I would rather not have to repeat. Once was enough.

DO NOT FEAR

Music and Lyrics by Olivia Ferguson

Before the earth was formed, I thought of you, My child:
Chose you, planning good works for you to do, My child.
And in your mother's womb I shaped you,
Gave you life, and breath, and made you my promise:
I will be with you.

Chorus
So do not fear, for I have redeemed you.
Do not fear—I have called you by name.
O, do not fear, though you walk through the fire.
Do not fear, do not fear, do not fear, My child.

I drew your heart to Mine, making you new, My child.
And on every battlefield, I've carried you through, My child.
So know, when night grows dark with weeping
Or test too great, I'm always keeping My promise:
I will be with you.

And when your race is run, I'll keep your hand, My child,
Share with you My joy in that far land, My child.
Safe in Christ you'll cross the river
And when your eyes awake forever, oh! then, child,
I will be with you!
You will be with Me.
I will be with you.

Bibliography

InvoCare Australia Pty Ltd. "Quotes." My Grief Assist, 2025. Accessed May 25, 2025. https://www.mygriefassist.com.au/inspiration-resources/quotes

Lucado, Max. *Safe in the Shepherd's Arms*. Edinburgh: Thomas Nelson, 2002.

MacDonald, James. *Always True: God's 5 Promises When Life Is Hard*. Chicago: Moody, 2011.

Stowell, Joseph M. *The Upside of Down*. Grand Rapids: Discovery House, 1991.

www.ingramcontent.com/pod-product-compliance
Lightning Source LLC
Chambersburg PA
CBHW061452040426
42450CB00007B/1332